FINANCIALLY FORWARD

ALEXA VON TOBEL, CFP®

FINANCIALLY FORWARD

HOW TO USE TODAY'S DIGITAL TOOLS TO EARN MORE, SAVE BETTER, AND SPEND SMARTER

CURRENCY

NEW YORK

Published in the United States by Currency, an imprint of
the Crown Publishing Group, a division of
Penguin Random House LLC, New York.
currencybooks.com

CURRENCY and its colophon are trademarks of Penguin Random House LLC.

Currency books are available at special discounts for bulk purchases for
sales promotions or corporate use. Special editions, including personalized covers,
excerpts of existing books, or books with corporate logos, can be created in large
quantities for special needs. For more information, contact Premium Sales at
(212) 572-2232 or e-mail specialmarkets@penguinrandomhouse.com.

Library of Congress Cataloging-in-Publication Data
Names: Von Tobel, Alexa, author.
Title: Financially forward : how to use today's digital tools to earn more, save better,
    and spend smarter / Alexa von Tobel.
Description: 1 Edition. | New York : Currency, 2019. | Includes bibliographical
    references and index.
Identifiers: LCCN 2018045519 | ISBN 9781984823526 (hardback) |
    ISBN 9781984823533 (eISBN)
Subjects: LCSH: Finance, Personal. | Finance—Technological innovations. |
    BISAC: BUSINESS & ECONOMICS / Personal Finance / General. |
    BUSINESS & ECONOMICS / Personal Finance / Money Management. |
    BUSINESS & ECONOMICS / Industries / Computer Industry.
Classification: LCC HG179 .V667 2013 | DDC 332.024—dc23 LC record available
    at https://lccn.loc.gov/2018045519

ISBN 978-1-9848-2352-6
Ebook ISBN 978-1-9848-2353-3

PRINTED IN THE UNITED STATES OF AMERICA

Book design by Andrea Lau
Jacket design by Lucas Heinrich

10 9 8 7 6 5 4 3 2 1

First Edition

To my children,
I'm excited for the possibility of the world you will live in.

To Cliff,
thank you for a lifetime's worth of love and support.

CONTENTS

I.

MODERN MONEY

II.

GET A PLAN

III.

HACK YOUR WALLET

IV.

THE FUTURE OF MONEY

FOREWORD

Meredith Kopit Levien,
COO of *The New York Times*

I first met Alexa in an elevator. We had both rushed breathlessly through its sliding doors, just before they clattered closed. It was that anxious hour between a busy workday and getting home to family, and we were racing to be on time for a reception welcoming the Aspen Institute's new class of Henry Crown Fellows.

Immediately, I could tell she was an original—from the way she dressed, to the way she talked, to the way she approached big ideas. By the time the reception was over, I knew I'd found a new friend—and, even though she's a decade younger than me, a new mentor.

I quickly came to appreciate that Alexa is as quick as she is thoughtful, a keen observer of the crowd, and a generous contributor to even the most taxing discussion—even discussions about taxes.

It's not that her core ideas about money are so unusual. It's the way she makes those ideas accessible. She has an uncanny sense for the things that people need to know but don't, and a peerless talent for communicating them through stories and experiences.

She's not the type of financial guru who traffics in get-rich-quick promises or tells you how to beat the market. Her mission—and method—is different. It's about empowering people with the means to live their most prosperous lives.

As a media executive, a parent, and a grateful friend, I share her fundamental belief that knowledge is power.

That's the mission I work on at *The New York Times*—to provide people with the knowledge they need to understand a fast-changing world. To persuade millions more people to spend much more time with quality journalism. Hers is to convince them to spend more time thinking about their financial future—how they can improve their lives, and the lives of their kids.

I grew up in a family where avoiding financial struggle wasn't a given. I saw firsthand the stress that comes from uncertain employment, and how financial literacy and discipline can be the antidote. My parents were relentless in their efforts to know more, save more, do more to claw their way to financial security. Ultimately, their dedication paid dividends; they found their financial footing and raised daughters who did the same.

When I think about Alexa's journey with LearnVest, I think first about the thousands of families whose lives she has impacted and improved. Families like mine, for whom understanding the tools at our disposal made a big difference in securing our best financial future. And how in *Financially Fearless* she decoded the basics from 401(k)s to student loan debt.

She could have stopped there, but like every other part of our lives, our relationship with money is rapidly changing. New technologies, new entrepreneurs, and new ideas are flowing into our daily lives. On a random Monday, you'll find me bouncing between Strava when I'm running, SI Play when I'm managing my son's soccer practice, and, of course, the *New York Times* app.

It's exciting, but with constant stimulation and so many sources of information, consumers want to be directed to what really matters.

That's why they turn to the *Times*, and I suspect it's why you picked up this book.

As Alexa shares in this book, we may well be on the cusp of a financial breakthrough, an evolution in money's status as inherently digital and tech-forward. This kind of innovation is compelling, but who has time to download the latest peer-to-peer money app or dig into the ins and outs of Bitcoin? As of this writing, there are 1,399 results for "Bitcoin" in *The New York Times* alone. There's a lot of news to sift through, which is why I love that Alexa has done all the heavy lifting for us. She's leveraged her decade-plus as a personal finance expert and Certified Financial Planner™, sprinkled in her business acumen with an eye on saving time and money, and spoken to her network of world-class experts to cut through the noise and tell us exactly what we need to know about the modern state of our bank accounts.

It's all too easy to ignore personal finance until it's too late. We all have a lot going on in our lives. Lord knows I do. My hope is that you dive into the pages ahead—taking advantage of how digestible Alexa has made these complex topics. I think there's something in here for everyone—old and young, money novices and experts alike—to live their best lives and prepare for their futures.

And by the time you're done reading, I know Alexa will feel like your mentor, too—no matter how old (or young!) you are.

Happy reading.

Today we are living in a new financial world. Our wallets—like every other aspect of our lives—are going fully digital. Technology is touching everything, and with these new advances come new opportunities for everyday Americans to maximize their money. A few big trends are impacting how we earn, save, invest, and manage our money in profound ways.

First off, we're living differently. From the gig economy to meaningful demographic shifts to sabbatical lifestyles, today there exist entirely different ways of funding our lives. The traditional 9–5 is no longer the only way to pay the bills. Technology gives us flexibility and freedom, but increasingly it's up to us to make our own job security.

Next, we're rapidly headed into a world of less ownership and more sharing. We use ride-share apps instead of owning cars, we rent Airbnbs instead of staying in hotels, we work in shared spaces instead of traditional offices. The idea of "ownership" is fluid, and today's digital tools make it easy and affordable to rent or lease just about *anything*.

You already know your time is money, but that idea takes on a whole new meaning in our on-demand world. As a wife and mom of two who also juggles a full-time, high-intensity job, I value every dollar and minute I put back in my life. Fortunately, gone are the days of having to brave crowded grocery stores or sit down with a stack of mail to pay the bills and balance the checkbook. From price alerts and delivery services, to auto-payments and money-tracking apps, technology has transformed how I spend and save—for the better—and it can for you, too.

Today we also use *far* less cash. Whether it's Apple Pay, Venmo, or Square, mobile pay is moving us further away from ever having to physically part with our money. That has a huge psychological impact on how we think about our wallets; we have to be more thoughtful about our spending when we don't hold cash in our hands and money is taken—invisibly and instantly—right out of our bank accounts. On the other hand, it's now instantaneous and virtually seamless to transfer money between people. Now we can track every expense down to the penny, and as ATMs become more obsolete, so do the fees. Plus, with brick-and-mortar banks falling by the wayside, it's far easier to pay our bills, apply for a loan or credit card, or even deposit a paycheck.

There's one other way in which money is going digital—literally. I'm guessing you've probably heard the hype about Bitcoin and other cryptocurrencies. Don't worry; if you're still a little (or more than a little) confused about how they work, you're not alone. I'll dig into the details of blockchain and cryptocurrency later in the book, but what's important here is to recognize that in the coming years blockchain and cryptocurrency might have the potential to change how we think about and interact with our money in all kinds of ways.

Of course, that we've entered the digital era is nothing new; after all, many of us can barely remember a time before the internet, and some of you might have been paying your bills online, or using a PayPal account, for close to a decade. But when it comes to our wallets, the move toward digital is stepping into overdrive.

I'll fully admit that I'm a geek when it comes to this topic, but how can I *not* be? We're living in an incredibly exciting time for financial technology. In fact, FinTech—the term for the rapidly growing sector devoted to using technology to improve our finances—is booming. There are hundreds of FinTech companies out there currently—working to find new and cutting-edge technologies to transform money from a source of stress to one of empowerment—and there are more popping up every day. According to a report from Pricewater-houseCoopers, venture capitalists have poured over $40 *billion* into FinTech start-ups since 2013.[1] FinTech encompasses many types of companies, but to understand the scope, consider the growth of just one small sliver: 264 payment-related start-ups have popped up in the United States since 1998, and those companies alone have received nearly $8 billion in investment dollars.[2]

The innovations that FinTech is driving are inevitable. But they're also very positive for us, American families trying to make the most of our money. There is a reason so much capital is flowing into the sector: investors, myself included, realize that today's technology offers ways to make your life easier and cheaper and put more money into your wallet. After all, technology already saves us time and headaches in every other area of our lives. It's time it did the same when it comes to money.

My hope is that my understanding of where our wallets are headed—and some of the tools I've picked up along the way—can help make you even savvier about how you earn, spend, save, and manage your money.

WHO I AM

But let's take a step back. How did I find myself at this new crossroads of money and technology? Those of you who have read *Financially Fearless* will be familiar with my story.

I was born in Kentucky and grew up in sunny Jacksonville, Florida. From a very young age, entrepreneurship was in my blood. Taking it up a notch (or five) from the classic lemonade stand, my earliest entrepreneurial venture was to set up an art fair—and no, I don't mean a refrigerator door display of the paintings I did at summer camp. I mean selling the artwork off my parents' walls!

From early on, my parents taught me to value being in control of my financial destiny. So at age ten, I got my first job, working in my dad's pediatric office. While I learned the ins and outs of filing and making photocopies, I also learned about the importance of saving for retirement. A few years into my first job, my parents started my very first Roth IRA, and my retirement planning began.

I guess you could say that being thoughtful about money is ingrained in my DNA. My dad's side of the family is made up of entrepreneurs who built successful companies of all shapes and sizes. My mom, on the other hand, comes from a very frugal, working-class background. My grandfather was a welder, and my grandmother was a phone operator at AT&T. When my mom was young, resources were limited but used strategically; her parents worked hard and bought everything in cash. So when I was growing up, my mom was incredibly intentional about her spending. We skimped on name-brand clothes and toys (we wore "peds" instead of Keds) but saved up to go on family vacations that opened our eyes to the world. My mom was an early adopter of the save-for-experiences-not-things mentality that I hold to this day—and that has become a proven approach to help you make the most of your money.

When I got to college, it hit me that money was a confusing topic for *everyone*—even my savvy Harvard classmates. My friends had no idea where to start when it came to budgeting and saving or even how to best pay down a credit card. But who could blame them? Personal finance is simply not taught in most schools around the country. The dual realization that (a) there was a massive education gap that needed addressing and (b) money is just math planted the seed for my start-up idea.

Fast-forward to 2008: after a few years of working as a trader at Morgan Stanley, I enrolled at Harvard Business School. Then the economy crashed. Lehman Brothers went under, and the conversations I had long been having with my peers about money suddenly took center stage, not just on Wall Street or in New York City, but on the front pages of newspapers, all over the internet, and in living rooms across the country. Suddenly *all* Americans were (rightfully) worried about how the recession would affect their livelihoods and families. That's when I realized that people were more desperate for a trusted source of financial advice than ever before.

So I did the logical thing and dropped out of business school (sorry, Mom!) to start LearnVest, a totally new kind of start-up that (I hoped) would disrupt the financial services industry for the better. LearnVest was all about using the tools of the digital era to make financial planning accessible and affordable for anyone—rather than just a luxury for the 1 percent—and because I believe in doing things fully, I even became a Certified Financial Planner™ myself. Eventually, I wrote the *New York Times* bestselling book *Financially Fearless*, with the goal of helping even more people make progress on their money.

In 2015, LearnVest was acquired by Northwestern Mutual, the storied 160-year-old Milwaukee-based insurance company that has a deep commitment to protecting its policyholders. The decision to partner with Northwestern Mutual wasn't just a smart move for my business; it was also deeply personal. When I was fourteen, my father suddenly passed away in an accident. Not only was it the most heart-wrenching tragedy my family ever experienced; it thrust my mom into the position of having to support our family, alone and for the first time. My mom was whip smart and money savvy but now found herself solely responsible for three children and all our finances. It was a horrible time, but we found stability thanks in large part to my dad's life insurance policy, issued by none other than Northwestern Mutual. That insurance policy didn't lessen our grief, but it did take one major source of stress—the question of how we would cope financially—out of the picture.

Sentimental attachments aside, joining forces with Northwestern Mutual was a no-brainer. For LearnVest, it was an opportunity to bring our financial planning software to millions more people nationwide. For Northwestern Mutual, rooted in an authentic commitment to help America's financial security, its visionary CEO, John Schlifske, saw it as a chance for us to team up and help more families in an even more powerful way. And for me personally, it was an opportunity to gain a new perspective on the industry in the role of Northwestern Mutual's first ever Chief Digital Officer, tasked with ensuring that we are constantly delivering cutting-edge financial services and keeping up with the rapid pace of change in the world around us.

Finally, because my enthusiasm for FinTech knows no bounds, I've been an active angel investor in the sector for five years now, which means I have had the opportunity to see some of the best and brightest ideas for how to modernize our wallets and to support some of the companies I think will help write the next chapter of our financial futures.

I consider myself lucky to have a job that fires me up in the morning and that feeds my deep passion for helping people feel more confident about their money. But at the same time, don't be fooled. I'm also a normal person, a wife, and a tired mom of two who struggles every day to find balance—to make enough time to do the things that are important to my career, spend time with the people I love, and stay sane along the way.

I'm far from having it all figured out, but there's one thing I know for sure: technology can help. I always say that money is simply a tool that was created to help us transact more easily. Well, the same can be said for financial technology. So in these pages, I plan to share with you everything I've learned as an entrepreneur, CFP®, and busy mom about how this tech revolution can help us maximize our time and our wallets.

WHY I CARE ABOUT YOUR WALLET

Money is deeply emotional for people. Through my work founding and running LearnVest, thousands of individuals have opened up to me about their tough financial situations. Parents who drained their retirement savings to send their kids to college. A woman whose fiancé broke things off at the eleventh hour, leaving her with both a broken heart and a mountain of credit card debt from wedding deposits that went unused. A recent college grad who had always dreamed of making a difference through nonprofit work but didn't know how to stretch his meager paycheck to make his rent. The list goes on.

Money is deeply personal, even existential, for many of us. In these turbulent times, it's natural to feel anxious about the future. We've all seen the headlines: the income gap is getting wider in this country—the bottom 40 percent of the country have an impossibly small sliver of wealth, while the top 1 percent have more than most people can imagine—which is why I care so deeply about providing tools and insights to help *all* Americans find stability. Will technology dislodge our jobs? Will the cost of health care become unmanageable? Will we be able to retire young enough—and with enough savings—to enjoy our golden years? When we are buried by the weight of financial stress—when we can't catch our breath or pay our bills—it's hard to be optimistic about what the future might bring.

I wrote this book because I believe that preparing ourselves for the financial future allows us to hope. To dream. It gives us dignity and security. And it gives us freedom.

If these are the things you want—for yourself, for your family, for the world—you've come to the right place. Whether you are a busy parent eager to learn how technology can save you money, time, and headaches, a tech-savvy millennial looking for tips to help you get more out of the tools you're already using, a near retiree trying to plan for your next chapter, or simply someone who realizes that these trends are the new normal but is struggling to keep up, this book will help you take full control of your future wallet. No matter your age, where you live, or what your finances currently look like, this book can help. I'll show you how to navigate all the ways in which technology is rewriting the rules, and walk you through how to use all the best (and simplest) new tools for getting more of your dollars. And I'll share all the proven best practices for keeping all your financial accounts, history, and data secure and safe in a digital world.

As always, this is a judgment-free zone. I believe the only way to make progress is in a safe space, focused not on the mistakes of the past (we all have them!) but instead on making your future brighter.

In the coming chapters, you will learn how to:

- ▷ put your savings—and spending—on autopilot;
- ▷ plan for the unexpected: everything from extra child- or elder-care costs to an adult gap year to a longer retirement;
- ▷ protect your identity, privacy, and hard-earned cash from getting into the wrong hands;
- ▷ talk to your kids (that is, digital natives) about financial planning;

▷ prepare for the potential future of blockchain and cryptocurrency.

Above all, this book will be chock-full of smart, simple, and jargon-free advice, tips, and strategies for managing your wallet in the digital age. Because, let's remember, the digital world is here to stay. It's time to move financially forward.

I

MODERN MONEY

CHAPTER 1

BUT FIRST, WHAT IS MONEY?

To understand how money is going digital, let's take a step back. If I asked you to visualize money, chances are you'd conjure up a picture of dollar bills (okay, maybe twenty- or hundred-dollar bills), some coins, or a shiny credit card.

But money didn't always look this way, and it won't always look this way in the future, either. If we're going to talk about the changing face of money, it's important to understand what counts as money in the first place.

WHAT MAKES MONEY, MONEY?

Merriam-Webster's definition of money is "something generally accepted as a medium of exchange, a measure of value, or a means of payment." More technical definitions evoke the same key qualities. To break it down, money is the following:

> ▷ **A MEDIUM OF EXCHANGE:** Money is something that can be used to facilitate an exchange of goods. It's a method of payment.
> ▷ **A STORE OF VALUE:** In and of itself, it maintains value whether I use it today or tomorrow (inflation aside).
> ▷ **A UNIT OF ACCOUNT:** Money can be used as a standard numerical unit to convey value.[1]

If you think about a dollar bill, you can see how it easily checks off those three qualities. You can exchange dollars for groceries, a dollar is worth the same amount whether you spend it today or if you pull it out of your wallet next week, and you know how expensive those groceries are based on the dollar amount assigned to them.

Experts vary in the exact number of characteristics, but there are six core ones to know, courtesy of the Federal Reserve Bank of Philadelphia:[2]

DIVISIBLE	Money must be easily divided into small parts so that people can purchase goods and services at any price.
PORTABLE	Money must be easy to carry.
ACCEPTABLE	Money must be widely accepted as a medium of exchange.
SCARCE	Money must be relatively scarce and hard for people to obtain.
DURABLE	Money must be able to withstand the wear and tear of many people using it.
STABLE	Money's value must remain relatively constant over long periods of time.

Why am I telling you all this? Because when we start to move beyond a physical dollar and think about where money will go digitally, these concepts quickly begin to feel abstract. We start to realize that money doesn't necessarily mean a piece of paper with a past president's face on it; it can be anything that displays a certain set of qualities. But before we get into any future forms money might take, I do want to walk through what economists consider the general evolution of "money" and how money came to look the way we know it today.

Back in the days of early human civilization, people relied on a **bartering** system. In ancient Mesopotamia (ca. 6000 B.C.),[3] I could trade you my cow for your grain, and because neither of those items was assigned a value, we determined their value ourselves. "Money" did not exist. We were directly exchanging the items we needed, and their value was based on how much we needed them and what we were willing to give for them.

Sounds nice and simple, but bartering actually came with all sorts of challenges. You had to find someone who had exactly what you were looking for, and when you found that person, you had to have exactly what he needed too. As you can imagine, this was not very efficient. So, money had to evolve.

Out of bartering emerged a solution: **commodity money,** which is just a fancy way of saying that any useful item with a fixed and agreed-upon value, like beaver pelts and gold, could be used as currency. Simply put, society shifted from trading the items they needed to trading items they could use to buy and sell other things (for example, instead of trading beaver pelts because they needed beaver pelts, people traded beaver pelts in order to buy other necessities).

There are many ancient examples of commodity money (these changes don't happen overnight): the anthropologist Chapurukha Kusimba points to the Mesopotamian shekel (that is, coin) used thousands of years ago, stamped silver and gold coins used in Asia Minor as early as 650 B.C., and the preponderance of metal coins used around the globe—from the Roman Empire to China—between 1250 B.C. and A.D. 1450.[4]

Advantages of commodities are that they are durable, portable, and

easy to store—some of the most significant and important characteristics of money.[5] But they have one significant downside: they exist in
finite quantities. And as populations grew, so did the amount of currency being transacted. Governments that wanted to put more money
into circulation couldn't simply print more gold or more beaver pelts the
way we do with dollars today. During the eighteenth century, colonial
governments mostly used paper money that was backed by commodities. But if they lacked common commodities, like gold, they instead
leveraged land-backed paper money. This money came out of so-called
land offices and allowed people to use their land as collateral (kind of
like a modern-day home equity line of credit, where you use your property value to access cash). Land offices, and the interest they collected,
took off in places like New York, Pennsylvania, and Delaware.[6]

In the United States, the next major evolution of money was **fiat
money**. Fiat money has value because a government declares it to be
legal tender, which explains the name: "fiat" means "it shall be" in
Latin.[7] In other words, fiat money is worth what our government has
decreed it to be worth. It is not backed by any physical commodity (a
paper bill is no longer a stand-in for a stash of gold sitting somewhere).
The value of a fiat dollar depends on the government's ability to regu-
late the currency.

The U.S. dollar became fiat in 1971, when Nixon moved us off the
"gold standard" (before 1971, the U.S. dollar could be redeemed for
gold, and the value of a dollar was tied to the value of gold).[8] In other
words, at just shy of fifty years old, the dollar as we know it today is a
small blip in the history of money.

But while the nature of money has evolved quite a bit over the
course of history, each new medium—bartering, commodities, fiat
money—was born out of essential needs that emerged over time.

I know this may all seem a bit academic, but here's why I think it
matters: I firmly believe that what we think of as *money right now* will
evolve—and *is already evolving*. If you look at history, it is only inevi-

table that our current definition of money is as fleeting as the $10,000 bills that were issued in the 1940s. Today's tech revolution is ushering in new forms of money that look nothing like any we have ever seen. Understanding the characteristics they share with the bills in your wallet can help you understand not just cryptocurrencies, but whatever unanticipated new modes of money the future may bring.

Innovations that shift our collective understanding of money aren't always quick to surface (though I would love for them to be, as an entrepreneur!). But since 1900, we've really picked up the pace. Checks and credit cards, for example, are shockingly recent inventions, and both are forms of money that took just decades to become completely ubiquitous.

Let's take a look at some of the major milestones that have transformed our definition of money here in the United States:[9]

KEY MONEY MILESTONES

1690	Massachusetts issues the first paper money in the United States.
1788	Congress establishes the dollar as the main unit of money across the country.
1863	National Bank Act passes; U.S. Department of the Treasury now oversees National Bank Notes, and state banknotes are pushed out of circulation.
1900	Gold Standard Act passes, which means the dollar is solely backed by gold.
1913	Federal Reserve is created.
1944	The World Bank is founded with an initial aim to help countries rebuild after World War II. Now it focuses on reducing poverty in developing countries.
1950	Diners Club becomes the first charge card, the early version of today's credit cards, inspired by a businessman's forgetting his wallet when out to dinner.

1969	Large-denomination bills—$500, $1,000, $5,000, and $10,000—are discontinued.
1974	Equal Credit Opportunity Act passes, allowing single women to take on debt without having a man co-sign.
1986	Sears launches the Discover card, one of the first credit cards to offer a cash-back rewards program.
1999	PayPal launches, though the original company name was Confinity, as a way to make payments via email. It gains traction over eBay, and as of 2018 PayPal boasts over 237 million active accounts.
2008	Lehman Brothers collapses, shaking the foundations of our financial system.
2008	Satoshi Nakamoto lays the foundation for blockchain, by describing a solution to the Byzantine Generals' Problem.
2009	Nakamoto mines the very first Bitcoins, launching the cryptocurrency into the world and beginning a craze that will take hold over the decade to come.
2010	Congress passes the Dodd-Frank Wall Street Reform and Consumer Protection Act, putting more safeguards in place for consumers via the creation of the Consumer Financial Protection Bureau.
2014	Apple announces Apple Pay, enabling consumers to make payments securely through their iPhones. A number of retailers sign on to accept Apple Pay at launch, including Whole Foods, McDonald's, and Duane Reade.

CHAPTER 2

SIX TRENDS CHANGING OUR WALLETS

When innovation is happening all around us, it's easy to lose sight of all the small ways in which technology is transforming our everyday lives. We now do things, on a daily basis, that would once have seemed like something from an episode of *The Jetsons* or some sci-fi movie set far into the future, like using a computer small enough to fit in your pocket to order dinner, hail a cab, and unlock your front door for the delivery guy when you aren't home; or walking around your house instructing "Alexa" to tell you the weather, reorder paper towels, and transfer $100 into a savings account.[1]

The point is sometimes it's easy to miss the change that's happening right under our noses. And today we're surrounded by macro-trends that are affecting how we live, some in more obvious ways than others. Let's break down what these trends are, why they matter, and what they mean for your wallet.

HOW WE LIVE

Trend 1: We're Living Longer
Trend 2: Our Family Structures Look Different

TREND 1: WE'RE LIVING LONGER

For every year that you live, you can expect to live longer. I know, it sounds like some mysterious ancient proverb, but here's the gist: human life expectancy is going up over time. We can make a broad assumption that on average people who turn thirty-five in 2030, for example, will have a longer life expectancy than people who turned thirty-five in 2029.

This trend has been around for a long time. As Laura Carstensen from the Stanford Center on Longevity explained in an interview with Fidelity,

> Life expectancy throughout most of human evolution was somewhere between 18 and 20 years . . . By the mid-1800s life expectancy had reached the mid-30s in the United States, and in 1900 it was 47 years. By the end of the century, life expectancy had reached 77. It gained 30 years in one century—that's unprecedented. *More years were added to average life expectancy in the 20th century than all the years added in all prior millennia of human evolution combined.*[2]

In today's world, American men can expect to live to 76.1, and American women to 81.1.[3] This doesn't just impact us individually; the age composition of our society is headed toward a big shift. By 2050, those who are 65 and up will represent 20 percent of the American population. One in five people might not seem like a huge number, but consider that the 65-plus demographic represented only 12 percent of the U.S. population back in 2000.[4]

The idea of age sixty-five marking the start of our "golden years" of retirement, which so many of us are wedded to, is a fundamentally modern concept. And it's a quickly evolving one. As our life spans extend, we need to adjust our financial plans accordingly. Here's how to think about the impact on our wallets:

WE GET MORE OF LIFE'S BIGGEST ASSET: TIME

Personally, I love this! Life is short—any trend that suggests we get *more* of it is what I'd consider a big positive. In fact, time is our biggest asset, and throughout this book we'll walk through some of my favorite tricks for maximizing yours. It's time to dream big for the years ahead, and this includes planning for a longer life span.

For whatever reason, though, we're not predisposed to think this way. Studies show that before we hit retirement age, the majority of us (two-thirds of men and half of women) underestimate the average life expectancy of a sixty-five-year-old.[5] This may sound like no big deal, but underestimating how long you might live can also mean underestimating how much money you'll need to live comfortably after you retire.

Another thing we forget to take into account is the fact that as we get older, our life expectancy goes up. The Social Security Administration (SSA) offers a helpful Life Expectancy Calculator that illustrates this point.[6] Take a 30-year-old woman, for example. The SSA puts her current life expectancy at 85.7 years. But once that woman reaches age 67, her expectancy rises to 88.9 years. By 70, that climbs again to 89.4. And remember, we're talking about averages here. That means many of us will live *longer* than the average and need to prepare for high odds that we—and/or our partners—will have a long, long life to live and fund!

It's not practical to plan for a life span that's down to the decimal, nor do I expect you to increase your retirement calculations every time you hit a birthday. But I do want to help you crystallize the idea that you should plan for a long life. Don't fall into the group of under-estimators. Think positive! And remember that the older you are, the older your life expectancy will be.

To be conservative, I recommend building your financial plan based on the assumption that you will live until at least ninety-five. Take your health and family status into account, too. If your parents or grandparents hit their centennial birthdays, assume you've also got those genes!

YOU MIGHT NOT RETIRE AT SIXTY-SEVEN (THE AGE WHEN SOCIAL SECURITY BENEFITS FULLY KICK IN)

For decades, sixty-five was considered the magic retirement age. If you can just hold out until then, it will be time to hit the beach and spend time with your grandkids. Why sixty-five? Mini history lesson: When our Social Security program was launched in 1935, the Committee on Economic Security (CES) had to lay out the ground rules. Existing state pension systems used two different retirement ages: sixty-five and seventy. Once it got into the nitty-gritty of actuarial studies, the CES decided that sixty-five was "more reasonable," and so that became the official retirement age across the board.[7] But then an amendment was passed in 1983 that raised the age at which someone could collect his or her full Social Security benefits from sixty-five to sixty-seven.[8] Now, if you were born after 1960, sixty-seven is the de facto retirement age.

Of course, that doesn't mean that you *have to* retire at age sixty-seven. In fact, a 2018 study by Northwestern Mutual found that 38 percent of Americans expect to retire *after age seventy*, while only 33 percent think they'll retire in their late sixties.[9] Why do people think they'll need to work longer? Money, of course. People are worried they simply won't have enough money in the bank to retire at sixty-seven, given how many years there are left in our expected life spans. What that means is more time in the workforce, but with a little bit of planning it also means more time to build that nest egg for when you do eventually retire.

It was totally reasonable for our grandparents to retire at sixty-seven. With lower life expectancies, they only had to fund a decade or so of retirement. But we're in a whole new ball game where we may need enough to live on for thirty-plus years. Luckily, the definition of "work" is also changing (more on that in a minute), which means lots more options and opportunities for supporting ourselves in those retirement years.

THE GIG ECONOMY MAY HELP

One of our biggest collective fears as a society is that we'll run out of money (especially with Social Security in question), so it's time to put aside the notion that these years should be spent at either extreme: all work or all play. In fact, the idea of a completely work-free retirement is a bit of a myth for today's retirees. Nearly one in five Americans over age sixty-five still works (at least part-time), and the Bureau of Labor Statistics (BLS) predicts that by 2024 over one-third of sixty-five- to sixty-nine-year-olds will be working—up from 22 percent three decades before.[10] And a full 79 percent of workers expect to supplement their retirement income through at least part-time work.[11] This is a big shift in how we think about our career longevity and what retirement even means.

I'm not telling you all this to cause alarm; personally, I can't imagine a scenario in which I wouldn't want to work, at least part-time. I know I'm not alone in saying that I am most motivated, inspired, and energized when I'm being productive and helping people around me. So why would I want to give that up entirely, even at age sixty-seven or seventy?

Carstensen agrees, noting that working longer is better for us both financially and psychologically. A Center on Longevity study found that people who continue to work have better cognitive performance than those who retire. There is no negative cognitive impact on those who take a break in their retirement years, but there is something about fully going into nonwork, permanent retirement mode that hurts our psyches.[12]

So it's no surprise that 40 percent of workers sixty-five and up are embracing flexible, part-time options like consulting, freelancing, coaching, and other gig economy work. Or that, according to the BLS, more and more older Americans are launching their own entrepreneurial ventures, with the BLS reporting that those in the sixty-five and older demographic are the most likely to be self-employed.[13] Bottom line: working a few extra years is good for our brains, and it's good for our wallets.

WHAT TO DO FOR YOUR WALLET

✓ GIVE YOURSELF OPTIONS.

I recognize that plenty of people may not *want* to work forever. Smart financial planning is all about having *options*. My hope is that you'll be in the position to choose whether you'd like to keep working. What better financial victory than getting to define what your dream retirement looks like?

✓ RUN YOUR RETIREMENT NUMBERS.

When you're figuring out how much you'll need for retirement, we use a retirement "replacement ratio" of 80–85 percent of your current salary. For example, if you make $100,000 per year currently, the idea is that you'll need at least $80,000 per year to live on during your retirement.

(Why not 100 percent? Because the metric assumes that some of your expenses, like mortgage payments and 529 contributions, will be a thing of the past.)

So, if you can expect to live an extra ten years, we're talking about saving and investing tens of thousands of extra dollars. I know—it's a staggering amount. But it's not as impossible as it sounds—as long as you start early. I'll go deeper into retirement savings in a later chapter, but the takeaway is that the earlier you're aware of how much you'll truly need for retirement, the sooner you can put a plan in place to take you there.

To predict roughly how many years you need to plan for, start by doing an assessment of your family history. At a bare minimum, plan to outlive your oldest grandparent by at least five years.

✓ VISUALIZE YOUR OLDER SELF.

Studies have shown that one of the reasons why it's hard to save for the future is that we're really bad at picturing our future selves. We see "the future self" as a stranger, someone distant and abstract.

There's fascinating research that shows people are inclined to save more for retirement when they can literally envision their older self. How much more? A Stanford study found that people who saw an aged avatar were willing to save *nearly twice as much money* for retirement.[14]

If you're having trouble visualizing what you'll look like at age one hundred, there are myriad new apps that help you do exactly that. Try running your picture through an app like FaceApp or AgingBooth, and picture "future you" the next time you make a 401(k) contribution.

TREND 2: OUR FAMILY STRUCTURES LOOK DIFFERENT

We all know the 1950s sitcom version of the average American family: husband and wife, picket fence, 2.5 kids. But when you take a look around, that's not the way most modern families look.

Our financial situation is inextricably linked to our family makeup, in a number of ways: Do you file your taxes as single or married? Are you financially responsible for a child or a parent? Do you have joint accounts with anyone? It's hard enough to tackle financial planning when you're the only person you have to worry about; try adding in someone else's circumstances, wants, needs, and so on, and suddenly things just got a lot more complicated. That's why a modern financial plan needs to take all of these factors into account.

But before we go into how (see chapter 3), let's look at *why* our family situations are getting more and more complex so we can better understand the forces that are impacting our wallets.

WE MARRY LATER

An increasing number of American couples are waiting to tie the knot. The numbers speak for themselves: on average, women get married (for the first time) at age 27.4 and men at 29.5.[15] Compare that with back in 1990, when the average age for women was 24 and for men, 26.1.[16]

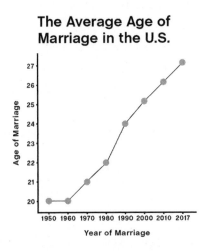

The Average Age of Marriage in the U.S.

Source: Macaela Mackenzie, "This Is the Average Age of Marriage Right Now: What's Your Guess?," *Women's Health,* March 26, 2018, https://www.womenshealthmag.com/relationships/a19567270/average-age-of-marriage

You don't need me to tell you that many couples live together—and even combine their finances—*before* they get married. This is a great way to get experience managing money as part of a couple, but marriage comes with a unique set of financial implications. To name a few: Married couples have a new tax status and the opportunity to take more deductions. If you're both working, you have double the health insurance options, and when it comes to retirement, you now have access to spousal IRAs.

"DINK" STATUS CAN BE GOOD FOR YOUR BANK ACCOUNT

Does being part of a dual-income couple mean more savings? Or more spending? Obviously the answer isn't the same for everyone, but according to data from the Bureau of Labor Statistics it turns out that on average combining your finances with a second earner leads to more money in the bank. The BLS estimates that single earners spend $40,438 annually, compared with $73,922 for a two-earner household. To break that down, couples spend $6,954 less per year, and each individual essentially holds on to nearly 10 percent more of their money.[17] If you invested that annual savings and socked it away for retirement every year, for forty years, that would amount to nearly $1 million ($882,043.71 to be exact).[18] So in short, pairing up is often good for your wallet.

In geeky financial-planning jargon, we call this status "DINK," which stands for "dual-income, no kids." It's a great place to be, financially, but it does come with a certain risk: with more money suddenly at your disposal, it can feel like you are rolling in it. But as tempting as it might be to start splurging on fancy dinners or a first-class upgrade on your next vacation, if you can use this time to ratchet up your saving (instead of spending), you have a huge opportunity to set yourself up well for the long haul.

WE HAVE MORE OPTIONS FOR STARTING FAMILIES

Science has given us more ways to start families on our own terms than ever before. As of 2015, more than seven million women in the United States had used fertility services, like IVF, and the Centers for Disease Control reports that nearly sixty-eight thousand babies in the United States are conceived via IVF each year.[19]

That said, it isn't cheap. While the cost of IVF was about $17,400 ten years ago, it's now closer to $21,000, according to Jake Anderson-Bialis, the co-founder of FertilityIQ. Then consider that the average IVF patient will cycle an average of 2.5 times. That brings the cost of having a baby via IVF to nearly $55,000.

Then there are the lingering costs when treatment is done. "Storing eggs and embryos often costs $1,000 per year, and for many reasons people rarely ever fully stop paying," explains Anderson-Bialis.

Although most insurance plans don't cover fertility treatment, there are options for managing these costs. Anderson-Bialis points to loans from companies like LendingClub and CapexMD, which "regard fertility patients as highly bankable and extend low APR loans. The carrying cost to the patient may be much lower than credit cards."

It's tough to put a price tag on the joy of bringing a child into the world, so it's never too soon to start putting money away to cover these costs.

THE COST OF RAISING A CHILD IS ON THE RISE

If you tally up the cost of raising a child these days—from food and housing, to child care—the "final bill" is sky-high. And it's growing. The USDA estimates that a child born in 2015 will cost families $233,610 from birth through age seventeen.[20] And that doesn't even include college.

Speaking of which, college tuition rates have been rising at about 4 percent per year, while the national inflation rate hovers around 2 percent.[21] Yes, that means tuition is increasing at nearly double the inflation rate. Ouch. Luckily, there are steps you can take to ensure that by the time your kids are ready to go off to college, you'll be prepared (financially, at least).

WE CARE FOR OUR PARENTS TOO, À LA "THE SANDWICH GENERATION"

It's no question that having kids—while wonderful and magical—puts a squeeze on your finances. And with Americans living longer, more and more of us are also being squeezed from the other side of the generational spectrum—our aging parents. There's a term for this phenomenon: "the sandwich generation."

Of course, not all of us will be financially responsible for our parents, but because it's impossible to know for sure what the future will bring, it's smart to be prepared. The first thing you should know is that the numbers around elder care are up there. Annual costs range from $47,928 a year for homemaker services (which include "hands-off" care, like cooking and cleaning) to $97,452 for a private room in a nursing home.[22] Unfortunately, Medicare and Medicaid may not be much help here. America's Health Insurance Plans estimates that 88 percent of the cost of nursing home care following a hospitalization falls on patients and their families.[23] One way to help offset costs? Long-term care insurance, which we'll tackle on page 89.

WHAT TO DO FOR YOUR WALLET

✓ **TALK TO YOUR FAMILY.**

Bringing up money with your parents and/or in-laws is not always easy, but it's critical. The goal is to understand if they're financially prepared and whether you might need to support them down the line.

✓ **PLAN FOR YOUR UNIQUE NEEDS.**

Think about what you want in your personal life. Who is currently in the picture? And what milestones might you hit in the coming years or decades that will impact your wallet? As we dive into the process of building a financial plan, keep this vision top of mind.

✓ PLAN WELL WITH OTHERS.

Understand that planning with another person takes everything up a notch. You're not just synthesizing your own wants, needs, and priorities but meshing those with someone else's. Work to create an open forum and healthy dialogue so that money is a positive conversation, no matter how complex the topics may be. And if you're in DINK territory, remember to save, save, save.

HOW WE WORK

Trend 3: Our Earning Power Is Flexible

Trend 4: Our Career Paths Are Fluid

TREND 3: OUR EARNING POTENTIAL IS FLEXIBLE (THANKS TO THE GIG ECONOMY)

For decades, "work" has been defined as a 9–5 job. People used to stick with one company for the long haul, and their earning power was determined by whatever that company was willing to pay them. But today, we now have massive flexibility around our incomes. With the rise of the gig economy, we are no longer at the mercy of any one employer. We can now literally monetize just about any unused time, on our own terms.

The "gig economy" is not just a buzzword. Thanks to technology that makes coordination easier than ever, this sector of work is growing by leaps and bounds. We often have a narrow view of what the gig economy entails, but it's not just about driving an Uber anymore. It's freelancers who prefer to jump from project to project, aspiring entrepreneurs with full-time jobs starting businesses on the side, professionals scratching their creative itch (while making money) via a side hustle, and everything in between. And it's had a tremendous impact on our collective wallets: gig workers have added an estimated $715 billion *annually* to the economy, according to a recent study.[24] Plus, an in-depth report by McKinsey found that a whopping 162 million people across the United States and western Europe partake in some form of independent work. That's more than one in four people!

Stacy Brown-Philpot, CEO of one of the most pivotal gig economy companies, TaskRabbit, explains,

> I think people thought [the gig economy] was this temporary thing that was going to get us through the recession in 2008. And here we are in one of the fastest-growing economies of our time, and the gig economy has essentially fueled that. It's really about the future of work. People are struggling to make ends meet. Most people live paycheck to paycheck and are one step away from poverty because a major bill happens. Your car breaks down. You lose your job. Someone gets sick, and you can't pay the bills. And all of a sudden there's the gig economy . . . That can help you make a few hundred dollars a month. And sometimes that's all you really need. It's the hope that people have for making ends meet. It's the flexibility to be able to pick your kids up from work. It's the opportunity to have pride in what you do.

The opportunity to impact your income outside your day job is one not to take lightly. As our lives change—we're juggling child care or trying to supplement our retirement income, for example—technology is empowering us to turn our free time into actual dollars.

SIDE HUSTLES COME IN MANY FORMS

The McKinsey report identified four main reasons people join the gig economy:

- ▷ **40 PERCENT** of independent workers do it for supplemental income. That captures everyone from families saving for a big purchase, like a house, to people simply looking for some extra discretionary cash.
- ▷ **30 PERCENT** are "free agents" who enjoy the flexibility of independent work and have opted to make it their primary income source, like a freelancer or full-time Uber driver.
- ▷ **16 PERCENT** are struggling financially and take on extra work out of necessity—like someone juggling multiple jobs and filling in the odd off-hour with a gig.
- ▷ **14 PERCENT** use independent work as their primary income source, like those "free agents," *but* would prefer a full-time role, if they could get one. Picture this as someone between jobs or still searching for a dream job.

THE BENEFITS ARE DIFFERENT

There's no doubt that the gig economy has its share of perks, like the ability to set your own schedule and hourly rate. But when it comes to the traditional, old-school benefits of employment—like a 401(k)—the rules are still being written.

When innovation occurs, it can take a while for the laws to catch up. Are gig workers employees of a company or merely independent contractors? The answer to that question—one that has been central to many recent legal debates—has a big impact on the financial benefits these workers can access.

When companies formally employ someone, they have to pay everything from workers' comp premiums to Social Security taxes. Plus, they're subject to a whole host of employment laws, like minimum-wage requirements. What that means is that employing someone is expensive, thanks to all these extra costs beyond just paying a salary. That's why many (not all!) companies that rely primarily on gig workers are set on ensuring that these workers remain "independent contractors." Doing so comes at a lower cost—both financially and in terms of liability.

What that means is that if gig work is your primary income source, you'll likely have to shoulder a couple of extra costs. First, health and dental insurance. This one is nonnegotiable: it's a requirement that everyone, and I mean everyone, no matter how young or healthy they are, be covered. And second, retirement savings. Without an employer-sponsored plan and automatic paycheck withdrawals, the onus falls to you to be proactive and diligent about saving. This is a real risk for far too many "full-time giggers." According to Betterment's 2018 report *Gig Economy and the Future of Retirement,* three in ten gig workers do not regularly set aside money for retirement.[25]

The gig economy isn't perfect, but it does allow us to write a new script for our careers and offer nearly limitless opportunities to supplement our incomes. I sincerely feel blessed that we live at a time when people can have this much flexibility for their wallets. That for me is huge progress.

YOUR TIME HAS MORE VALUE THAN EVER BEFORE

In *Financially Fearless,* I shared a simple calculation to help you figure out what your time is worth. You simply divide your monthly take-home pay by the hours you work each month to uncover your hourly rate. Why does this matter? Because, often, saving money takes time—like the thirty minutes you spend on the phone with your credit card company to dispute a charge. So knowing the value of your hour helps you decide whether spending your time to save money is worthwhile.

Before the gig economy, that equation was purely conceptual. Would I tell you it's a good idea to spend ninety minutes on hold waiting to talk to someone about a $6 charge? Almost certainly not. Still, it was unlikely that someone would actually pay you for that time, particularly if you're someone who collects an annual salary and doesn't qualify for overtime.

But in the gig economy, you *can* monetize that hour if you choose to, and it can transform your financial life. According to Brown-Philpot, people earn, on average, $35 per hour using TaskRabbit—which is five times the federal minimum wage. If someone works just fifteen hours a week, that amounts to bringing home an extra $2,100 each month. As Brown-Philpot sees it, "That gives people the opportunity to invest, save, pay bills, and provide for their families in a way that works for them."

WHAT TO DO FOR YOUR WALLET

✓ **FIGURE OUT HOW THE GIG ECONOMY CAN HELP YOU REACH YOUR GOALS.**
Are there things you want to do that your current financial status is holding you back from, like taking a

vacation or accelerating loan payments? Use the gig economy to your advantage. Think about everything you could possibly do on the side. Most of us have at least one hobby that we can turn into a source of income, given the endless gig apps out there.

Can you drive? Grocery shop? Pet sit? Hang art? There's an app that will pay you for that (see Lyft, Instacart, Rover, Handy). And sites like Fiverr, Upwork, and TaskRabbit all offer a wide range of freelance opportunities, everything from web design to copywriting to event planning. You can find a full list of resources and apps on page 184.

✓ WANT TO BE A FULL-TIME "GIGGER"? MAKE SURE TO DO THE MATH.

If you're transitioning into gig economy work, there are a number of things to consider (outside the income you could rake in). Essentially, you have to zero in on not just what you earn but your net salary (revenue minus expenses, including taxes). Make sure you understand both self-employment taxes (paid quarterly), where retirement contributions fit in, and how much health-care insurance will cost. Not to mention that there's often a cost of doing business, like gas and car maintenance as a ride-share driver, or fancy equipment as a video editor, and so on.

✓ UNDERSTAND YOUR IDEAL TIME COMMITMENT.

While taking on gig work might seem like a no-brainer, do think through the time you have available and what you'd need to bring in for a freelance hour to make that worthwhile for you. That number will be different for each of us. For many of us, spending some of our evenings or weekends to increase our earnings is hugely worth it. Not only does it help our wallets, but it gives us something meaningful to do with our time. One great example of a gig economy company is the start-up Umbrella, which helps connect older people with handy workers who can tackle the chores that become insurmountable with age.[26]

TREND 4: OUR CAREER PATHS ARE FLUID, AND SABBATICALS ARE IN

It's the eternal question posed to new college grads, "What do you want to do with your life?" The formula used to be super simple, and it goes back to the retirement math of trend 1. Just a few generations ago, you would pick your career, work for a company or two, retire at sixty-five, collect your pension, and enjoy your last few decades.

That was really the only option that existed for my maternal grandfather, who came from a hardworking, blue-collar family. He served in the army and then worked for forty years. In short, he got two weeks of vacation a year plus holidays, and at sixty-five he was given the option to retire. Luckily, his health was amazing, and we got to enjoy such phenomenal time with him through his ripe old age of eighty-seven.

Today, however, we live in a fundamentally more flexible era, thanks to economic and cultural shifts that force us to be more flexible around work, and technology that enables us to do so.

We look at our careers in a fresh way: making a "career move" used to mean moving up the corporate ladder at the same company, but today we're quite amenable to job-hopping. In their first five years out of college, people who graduated between 2006 and 2010 worked for twice as many companies as people who graduated between 1986 and

1990.[27] In addition, 64 percent of people surveyed in 2018 think that changing roles every few years is a smart career move—a 22 percent increase from 2014.[28]

Second, we're not just open to changing companies; we're also open to changing our careers. Nearly eight in ten twentysomethings said they were in the market for a career change, and 54 percent of fortysomethings feel that way too.[29] And 40 percent of Americans still working at age sixty-two had made a career shift sometime after age fifty-five.[30] There's no such thing as it being "too late" to pursue an entirely new path.

All of this job-hopping and career swapping has led to people getting savvier about the time they take off from work. There's an entire generation of millennials who are questioning why they would save up all of their downtime for their sixties or seventies when they may be in questionable health.

I've witnessed a truly exciting trend: people are now taking more time off in between jobs (when the temptation to read work email or check in with colleagues is nonexistent) or taking full-blown sabbaticals from their current one. My stance on the sabbatical trend is that it's phenomenal. Getting to enjoy your life to the fullest when you know you're able to is a huge win.

That said, you have to plan for it, and you of course need to pay for it. The dream here is to be able to take a step back from the day-to-day grind without draining your bank account or tanking your career. I think it's possible, but here's what you need to know.

INTEREST IN SABBATICALS IS ON THE RISE

Back in 2009, Stefan Sagmeister gave a TED talk that has since been viewed over three million times.[31] In it, he explains why he takes a year-long sabbatical from his design studio work every seven years, and in the process he validates a brilliant way to fit sabbaticals into your working life. Sagmeister explains, "Right now, we spend about the first twenty-five years of our lives learning, then there [are] another forty years that [are] really reserved for working, and then tacked on to the end of it are about fifteen years for retirement . . . I thought it might be helpful to basically cut off five of those retirement years and intersperse them in between those working years." That vision looks something like this:

LEARNING	WORKING	RETIRING

| 0 | 25 | 69 | 80 |

Source: Stefan Sagmeister, "The Power of Time Off," TED Talk, July 2009, https://www.ted.com/talks/stefan_sagmeister_the_power_of_time_off

In addition to the large audience that has flocked to Sagmeister's TED talk, another great indication that people are intrigued by the possibility of a sabbatical is found in Google's Trends tool, which measures how often we search for certain key words. Consider how "time off from work" has continued to climb over the last decade, more than tripling in popularity from 2008 to 2018.

Jan 1. 2008   Feb 1. 2011   Mar 1. 2014   Apr 1. 2017

Source: Google Trends

Not to mention that the term "adult gap year" turns up 122 million Google search results, or the fact that Tim Ferriss's *4-Hour Workweek*, which extolls the virtues of a sabbatical lifestyle, spent months and months at the top of the best-seller lists.

It's easy to see why the idea of ditching the cubicle life for a few months to travel the world would be glamorous, but is it practical? Increasingly, yes.

EMPLOYERS ARE GETTING ON BOARD

"Taking a break" used to be considered irresponsible—something associated with surfers and slackers—but luckily the stigma is lifting. In fact, these days, instead of being deemed a career killer, sabbaticals are being lauded as a boon for both your individual growth *and* the health of your career.

What's changed? Well first off, companies and employers are finally recognizing that taking time off from work has countless benefits. For one thing, it's a chance to broaden our horizons by cultivating new skills or interests and learning from other cultures. Plus, when we're recharged, we're more creative, innovative, and, most important, motivated and productive.

A sabbatical is just an extended vacation from work, and the benefits of vacation are not just hype. Research from Project: Time Off found that taking time off dramatically increases the likelihood of getting a raise or bonus. Employees who used fewer than ten vacation days annually had a 34.6 percent chance of a raise or bonus over a three-year period, compared with a 65.4 percent chance for those who took more than ten days.[32]

While universities have long offered sabbaticals to give professors a chance to regroup and even dig into research, we are now seeing a growing number of companies recognize that a little break can lead to more-engaged employees.[33] As of 2017, the Society for Human Resource Management found that about 17 percent of employers offer a sabbatical (paid or unpaid). There are many companies at the forefront of this trend: Zillow offers up to six weeks off for every six years an employee works (half of which is paid), and Charles Schwab gives employees a twenty-eight-day break on their fifth work anniversary.[34] Overall, nearly one-fourth of Fortune 100 companies offer some sort of time-off program.[35]

WHAT TO DO FOR YOUR WALLET

✓ CHECK YOUR COMPANY'S POLICY.

If sabbaticals or extended time off from work are appealing to you, see what your company already offers. If a break kicks in after you hit a certain employment anniversary, that may be added incentive not to job-hop if a sizable amount of PTO is within reach.

✓ MAKE A SOLID PLAN.

If you want to take breaks in your career—be it longer vacations or a full-blown sabbatical—you'll need to do some major financial planning. Maybe you work to reach tenure at your company so it gives you time off that's paid. But what if you determine that you want to take a year off between jobs to travel the world? This is likely going to require trade-offs in your budget. But the good news is that *you* get to choose where that money comes from; perhaps you don't eat out as often, or decide to rent out or Airbnb a room in your home. In addition to budgeting for a year of living expenses, account for a year in retirement savings. Your sabbatical may well turn out to be an amazing once-in-a-lifetime experience. My job is to help make sure you can pay for it.

HOW WE SPEND

Trend 5: Everything is on-demand.

Trend 6: Forget ownership. Sharing is the new
economy.

TREND 5: EVERYTHING IS ON-DEMAND

The fact that on any given day I can have just about anything delivered
to my home on-demand is probably one of the best perks of the digital
era in which we all now live. The instant, on-demand economy saves
me travel, time, hassle, and money, and I want everyone reaping the
same benefits.

My appreciation for this world of instant gratification is particularly heightened as a working mom. Over the past few decades, there
has been a massive proliferation of apps that put access to the things
you want to buy right into the palm of your hand, using technology to
instantaneously match those seeking a product or service with those
who provide it in real time.

ON-DEMAND IS AVAILABLE FOR JUST ABOUT ANYTHING

When you think about "on-demand," your mind likely jumps right to
Uber. You pull out your phone to let Uber know you need a ride; it
finds the closest available driver to solve that need and then sends him
or her to your door—often in ten minutes or less.

Uber might have been one of the first, but today a whole host of
companies has reimagined the consumer experience on a broader
scale. What's most impressive about on-demand's potential is its
scope. Nothing seems to be off-limits. There's an explosion of compa-

nies bringing your favorite meal right to your door, from Postmates to DoorDash to Grubhub to Minibar. We're talking about not just sushi and burgers but groceries too, thanks to Instacart, which will deliver from any grocery store in your area. Then there are subscription services like Blue Apron, Plated, and HelloFresh that will bring recipes and the pre-portioned ingredients you need to make them right to your doorstep. You can order an in-home massage (Zeel) or a manicure and blowout (Glamsquad). You can even have your bed made (Handy) or light bulb changed (TaskRabbit). And you can binge-watch just about any TV show or watch every movie (Netflix, Hulu) from the comfort of your own living room (bonus: popcorn at home is much cheaper than at the theater).

Technology has lowered the barrier of entry for these new businesses, which is why they abound everywhere you look. The upside to all this competition, for now at least, is that competition tends to keep prices lower for consumers.

WE HAVE *FAR MORE* OPTIONS AT FAR LOWER PRICE POINTS

One of the best things about all of these on-demand options is that they put choice in the hands of the consumers. Think about feeding your family. Our options used to be limited to either eating out or grocery shopping and then cooking at home. On-demand has expanded your options not just to takeout but to an entirely new category of "meal kits" delivered right to your door, allowing you to make a home-cooked meal—usually designed to be prepared in thirty minutes or less—without the hassle of shopping for or measuring out ingredients. This simple shift provides an immense win for the average family. As Matt Salzberg, founder and executive chairman at Blue Apron, says, "I think consumers win when there's more choice. It's about consuming only what you need and not wasting money on things you don't . . .

We're re-portioning ingredients to only sell you exactly what you need so there's no waste." He has a point. We all end up tossing out some percentage of our grocery bill each week—money that could otherwise be working for us.

The rise of the on-demand economy has introduced entirely new business models that let us spend our money in new ways. Our choices—DIY or full-service experience—are no longer binary, and this doesn't just go for cooking. Whether it's a home renovation or a freelance project that proves more time-consuming than we bargained for, on-demand allows us to get the help we need, when we need it, so we can maximize the return on investment of our time.

And, this new way of consuming opens up a massive opportunity to better compare prices. Let's say you need a new lawn mower. It used to be, you get in the car, you drive to the hardware store, and you have a few options to choose from. Maybe it had a brand on sale, but it sold out of them. Oh, well.

Today, you can go online and comparison shop from hundreds of stores and sort through thousands of items *instantly*. And then! You can have the best and cheapest option delivered straight to you, likely with free shipping! Technology has given us endless options—along with price transparency, which means that now you know how much not only your local hardware store charges but all the top retailers across the country. That's more power, and more savings, in your hands.

ON-DEMAND SERVICES SAVE YOU TIME AND BOOST YOUR HAPPINESS

The value of on-demand companies goes beyond cost saving. It saves us time too.

You might have heard that studies have shown that we're happier when we spend on experiences rather than on things. Harvard Business School professor Michael Norton is one of the pioneers of that research, and I asked him whether technology has enabled any new ways for us to "buy happiness." The answer is a resounding yes.

Norton points to new research led by Ashley Whillans that reveals that "using money to buy time—like paying someone to clean your bathroom or for an hour of child care—reduces our feelings of time stress and allows us to spend time on the activities, and with the people, we love."

It turns out that the trade-off we make for many on-demand products and services—money for time—is a valuable one. Having worked in Harvard's "Happiness Lab," I'm thrilled to know that the research backs up what I've found to be true in my own life. We may feel reluctant to outsource our to-do lists, but when you're weighing how to allocate your dollars, consider investing here. As the lead researcher, Whillans, puts it, "The more stressed you feel, the less control you feel over various components of your life . . . Money is a tool that allows you to purchase that control."[36]

WHAT TO DO FOR YOUR WALLET

✓ PARTICIPATE IN ON-DEMAND.

Guess how many Americans shopped online back in 2000? Only 22 percent. As of 2016, that number had jumped to nearly 80 percent.[37]

But participation in the on-demand economy is still relatively low. For example, only 4 percent of Americans have hired someone online to do an errand for them, according to Pew research.[38] Many more Americans are taking advantage of same-day delivery (41 percent), but they are not yet extracting the full value from on-demand's varied offerings. Think about what additional on-demand services you could use to save time, money, and hassles in your own life. (And if you don't live in a big city, these options are still available to you! In fact, 39 percent of on-demand consumers currently live in small towns.)[39]

✓ LOOK FOR COST SAVINGS IN NEW AREAS OF YOUR BUDGET.

Because on-demand options are so ubiquitous, you can find a way to leverage them in just about every part of your budget. Once you have your budget in place (see page 68), go through and identify places to save money and increase convenience.

For example, the tried-and-true tip of cutting your cable is so much less painful thanks to the on-demand economy. Now, instead of cable versus no cable, you have the option of subscribing to streaming services like Hulu and Netflix—both more affordable than a traditional cable package. Moving from cable to streaming is such a trend there's even a name for those who have taken this step: cord cutters. So cut the cord, and stop paying good money for entertainment you can get elsewhere at a fraction of the price.

✓ BE THOUGHTFUL ABOUT IMPULSE BUYS.

On-demand apps get a high mark for convenience, but remember that these costs can add up. It's easy to see why we're putting a lot of our dollars here. On-demand apps give us a constant opportunity to impulse buy, just as long as we have a smartphone in hand. And with more and more companies offering same-day shipping, it's only getting more and more tempting. Google search data reveals that more and more people—over 120 percent more between 2015 and 2017[40]—are searching "same-day shipping" in the morning so that they can have items delivered to their doorstep by the time they get home.

In 2016, researchers estimated that we collectively spend over $57 billion in the on-demand economy.[41] Knowing that the on-demand economy isn't going any-where—if anything, it's only expanding into new prod-ucts and industries—we have to learn to pause and ask ourselves, "Do we really need this service or item?" There are many pros of clicking on that "confirm purchase" button—convenience, cost savings, and instant grati-fication. Just make sure you're making these purchases thoughtfully and weighing them against your budget.

TREND 6: FORGET OWNERSHIP. SHARING IS THE NEW ECONOMY.

Remember that idea of the American Dream I mentioned when we talked about the modernization of the family unit? Well, core to that concept is ownership. In the past, it was assumed you'd not only have 2.5 kids and a picket fence but also own your dream home—with lots of closets packed with both needs and wants, and a shiny new car parked in the driveway.

But something big is happening: *We don't need to own that much stuff anymore.*

This is great news given how expensive ownership is. When my husband and I got married and combined our stuff, there were still many things we didn't have—like a blender or a tool kit. At the time, these seemed like perfect items to add to our wedding registry. But when I look back, I realize that we didn't need to accumulate all that stuff, just to have it, or to feel like "grown-ups." I could have borrowed a hammer from our neighbor to hang photographs on the walls or rented a blender through an app.

The point is, sometimes, it just doesn't make sense to own. And I'm not just talking about tools and kitchen gadgets. Depending on where you live and how frequently you drive, for example, it may be far more expensive to own a car than to use ride-share services. Likewise, if you are someone who wants to be wearing the latest fashion each season, it's probably cheaper to rent a closet's worth instead of buying it. And if you're a movie aficionado, why spend your hard-earned cash on a movie collection when you can stream as many new movies as your heart desires without ever clicking "purchase"?

Back in 2011, *Time* magazine ranked "sharing" as one of the ten ideas changing the world.[42] To see how far we've come since then, consider Airbnb. Fifteen years ago, if I told you that it would become perfectly normal to go into a stranger's house, sleep in their bed, cook in their kitchen, and use their shower, you would have thought I was crazy. As of 2017, Airbnb has a valuation of $31 billion, which makes it twice as valuable as Hilton and nearly as valuable as Marriott.[43] In August 2018, Airbnb hit a milestone, with 3.5 million people staying in strangers' homes on a single night.

From bikes to ski equipment to handbags to parking spaces, these days there's a sharing app for just about anything. And I believe that this trend—pay to use the things you need, when you need them—is only gaining more and more momentum.

Here are some of the ways this is playing out and how it can put money back into your pocket.

WE ARE SPENDING LESS ON "STUFF"

Here's a statistic that might shock you: the average American home contains *more than 300,000 items*.[44] Yes, you read that number correctly. And the implications are clear: we Americans have a serious clutter problem. But if the breakout success of Marie Kondo's mega best seller *The Life-Changing Magic of Tidying Up*—and the decluttering craze it spawned—are any indication, we are now finally beginning to ask ourselves, how much of this stuff do we actually want or need?

What we as consumers value has evolved. A 2012 study in the *Journal of Consumer Research* argues that in today's world "consumers want access to goods and prefer to pay for the experience of temporarily accessing them. Ownership is no longer the ultimate expression of consumer desire."[45]

And according to a 2014 report from Eventbrite, "Since 1987, the share of consumer spending on live experiences and events relative to total U.S. consumer spending increased 70%."[46] In other words, people prefer to spend on experiences rather than more stuff, and the sharing economy has given us more freedom to put our dollars where our wants are.

When we own less, there are three big wins: First, our carrying costs go down. Maintaining stuff is expensive! So is fixing things when they break or replacing them when they get ratty and worn. Second, we have a more streamlined lifestyle. Our closets—and arguably our minds—become less cluttered. And third, every dollar that you're not spending on an item sitting unused in your garage can be working for you in the markets.

WE GET ACCESS TO THE LATEST AND GREATEST

Wish you could afford a high-end camera, a designer wardrobe, or a boat? The sharing economy puts those things within reach—temporarily at least. In this new world, the economic equation is clear: consumers can get higher value at a lower cost.[47] As Jennifer Hyman, CEO and co-founder of Rent the Runway, puts it, "The sharing economy democratizes industries into all-you-can-eat buffets."

It's true: the sharing economy gives us access to much more choice. Max Motschwiller, a general partner at Meritech Capital Partners whose investments focus on consumer companies, gives a great example around the future of ride-sharing apps. Motschwiller believes that if ride-sharing companies realize their vision, they could shift to a subscription model that would entitle customers not just to rides but to on-demand access to various modes of transportation: a ride-share car, a rental car, a bike, an e-scooter, and even access to public transportation. And, the app would instantly recommend which mode of transportation to take, based not just on your location and destination but also on traffic patterns, time of day, your personal preferences, and even the weather.

And just like that, transportation could transform overnight. Not only does this mean we always have transportation at our fingertips; it means we also have the *best* mode of transport at our fingertips.

More value, and more choice, for less money are overwhelmingly positive developments for our collective wallets.

WE CAN BENEFIT FROM BOTH SIDES OF THE SHARING EQUATION—WE CAN MAKE MONEY BY SHARING OUR STUFF, TOO

As the above examples show, owning less can be a financially savvy move. Taking this one step further, the sharing economy creates all kinds of opportunities to increase the value of the things we already own.

The sharing economy is closely linked to the gig economy and on-demand economy in that it opens up a new way of thinking. It allows us to ask the question, can I get any value out of stuff I already own?

Airbnb hosts, for example, set their own listing prices and keep up to 97 percent of what they charge, says Kim Kingsley, director of global communications for Airbnb. "The typical U.S. Airbnb host is middle-class and shares their home around forty-three times a year, three to four days a month, and earns $7,500 in additional income, which is the equivalent of a 14 percent raise." As consumers, we have so many more levels of choice with Airbnb outside the traditional realm of hotels. Plus, Airbnb connects us to real people. It makes us feel good to put money into our hosts' pockets and to put our hard-earned dollars toward a family that likely needs it. The economic benefits to hosts are powerful.

A 14 percent raise has a real impact on our wallets. If you own a home with an extra room, a car you never drive, or even some old sporting equipment gathering dust in the garage, the sharing economy can empower you to make your own financial picture that much brighter.

WHAT TO DO FOR YOUR WALLET

✓ **DECIDE WHAT YOU ACTUALLY NEED TO OWN.**

Before buying anything, ask yourself how often you will realistically use it, and then find out how much it would cost to "share" or rent. Then do the simple math to figure out whether owning it even makes sense. Remember, cutting back on things you own will put extra funds back into your financial plan to deploy elsewhere.

✓ **IDENTIFY THINGS THAT YOU CAN SELL OR SHARE.**

One of the best outcomes of the sharing economy is the secondary market for all of our stuff. Take a look at all the stuff you own and figure out how to extract more value from it, like posting old clothes on a resale site. Thanks to sites like The RealReal and Tradesy, you can remonetize everything that's sitting in your closet unused, and that means more money in your wallet.

II

GET A PLAN

CHAPTER 3

THE FINANCIAL FOUNDATION EVERYONE NEEDS

When I founded LearnVest, there was one question I was asked time and time again from thousands of users. "What should I do with my next dollar?" They wanted what we all want: to maximize their money and feel that they were making good decisions. So my advice to them was always the same: you have to get a financial plan.

For most of us, a "financial plan" isn't a term that necessarily evokes huge excitement. It sounds daunting, like homework. Or we assume it's something that doesn't really apply to us: something for the 1 percent. Or something overly complex. But when you boil it down, a financial plan can be short and simple enough to fit on a single page. Think of it less like homework and more like a road map that helps you understand what your money situation looks like today and how you're going to reach your financial goals.

With the world changing as quickly as it is, having a current financial plan that reflects the trends transforming how we live, work, and spend is a must. It's something we all need to have, regardless of age, income level, or anything else. As I like to say, not having a plan *is* a plan—just a really, really bad one.

As John Schlifske, CEO of Northwestern Mutual, puts it, "People need a financial plan that prepares them for all economic seasons. No hot stock tip can save the day if you haven't done thorough financial planning with a focus on saving and protecting yourself from risks. A relentless focus on following a strong financial plan will protect you more than any [other] advice you'll ever get."

We are so fortunate to have access to more digital tools that help us manage our money better than ever before. It's up to us to optimize these tools and incorporate them into a modern plan, for our modern wallets.

So let's do this, CliffsNotes-style. Here are the seven steps to a financially forward plan.

STEP 1: GET DIGITALLY ORGANIZED

Let's start at the beginning. The goal here is to ensure you know where all of your accounts are before you dive into the worthwhile process of putting everything in one spot.

Luckily, there are a ton of new tools out there to help you up-level your money-organization skills.

TAKE INVENTORY

Knowing *where* all of your money is and in what form—from cash under your bed to old 401(k)s you forgot to roll over from your last job—is the first step to getting a handle on where you stand.

Ideally, you already have a thorough list of where your money sits. Run through the obvious suspects (checking and savings accounts, credit cards, your retirement fund through your current employer); then consider whether you might have any accounts that you've forgotten about, like an old department store card from a decade ago buried in a drawer or any old 401(k)s from prior jobs.

I also want you to think about any tangible assets you have, like jewelry, electronics, or cars. Anything with a sizable resale value counts. We'll account for it all!

PRO TIPS

- Unsure what lines of credit might be out there in your name? Go to AnnualCreditReport.com, download your free report, and it will give you a full breakdown of what's currently associated with your name and Social Security number.
- Let's say you forgot about a childhood checking account or (for some reason) didn't claim the entirety of your tax refund. You probably thought that cash was gone forever, right? But there are now websites where you can find "unclaimed money"—dollars owed to you by the government or by a bank. The usa.gov site is a good place to start reclaiming any cash that is rightfully yours.

CREATE YOUR DIGITAL SETUP

Yes, the internet is here to stay! If you're reading *Financially Forward*, chances are that you understand the incredible benefits of going digital with your money. If you're feeling skeptical of online security, know that modern encryption technology and other safeguards—like facial-recognition technology on our phones—get smarter and more secure every day.

Now that you know what money you have and where, it's time to build and customize your money-management system. Here are a few simple, one-and-done actions that will pay dividends (if not in actual dollars, then in time, peace of mind, and convenience!). Getting organized is like a gift that keeps on giving.

> **PICK AN APP.** There are a number of personal financial management apps (or PFMs, as they're known in the FinTech world) that will link all your accounts so you can view your money in one spot. Do a quick Google search (or go to page 186 for a list of my personal recs), and choose the one that suits you best.

Side note: Yes, you should confirm that the PFM follows security best practices, but note that most simply provide a window into your finances. They're not hubs to actually move money around.

> **IF YOUR WALLET IS GOING DIGITAL, IT'S GOING TO NEED AN EMAIL ACCOUNT.** Perhaps my all-time favorite tip is to set up a separate email account just for your money (think: alexasbills@gmail.com). This ensures your financial docs are all in one spot, so nothing gets buried or lost. Make sure to update your new email address across your bank accounts, so that all relevant docs go to the right place. This is also a great way to get organized and share key money info with your partner or spouse.
> **GO GREEN.** There is literally no reason you should be getting credit card bills and bank statements in the mail anymore. At a basic level, going paperless means you can log in to your account online, receive statements via email, and make payments digitally. It's good for the planet, and it saves you the hassle of physically filing away all your documents.
> **RUN YOUR FINANCES THE WAY YOU RUN YOUR SOCIAL LIFE.** Managing your calendar is serious business. We've gotten so used to

getting digital reminders for everything—from work meetings to doctors' appointments to social engagements—why not set up a reminder for your credit card payment due date or a reminder to check your credit score every three months, just as you would for remembering your best friend's husband's birthday? Set up calendar reminders for your money to-dos, like you do for your work and personal reminders. Not sure what dates to add? Head to page 119 for a full calendar breakdown.

▷ **STORE KEY DOCS IN THE CLOUD.** If you have other financial docs lying around that aren't yet digitized, bringing them into the cloud can be as simple as taking a picture on your phone. Consider keeping important docs in a folder on your phone—so long as your phone is thumbprint/face ID/password protected (today's smartphones often automatically back up all their files using cloud-based storage, so even if you lose your phone, you won't lose these files). Phone technology has come a long way, so let's use it.

SIMPLIFY YOUR ACCOUNTS

As you do the work of getting organized, you might discover that you have *a lot* of accounts to track. It's time to simplify. That checking account you've had since college? The credit card that got you the airline points you used for your last big vacation . . . in 2010? It's time for those to go.

So how many accounts is the right number of accounts? I'm a firm believer that in a perfect world, you'd have accounts with no more than two or three financial institutions (banks and brokerages), and no more than two or three credit cards (ideally with the same banks). Limiting the number of financial institutions you work with helps save you time because it means fewer log-ins when you want to check balances, move funds, or cash in on benefits like credit card points.

When you have tons of financial accounts scattered across different banks, keeping track is a major headache. It's kind of like having kids: one is easier than two, and two is easier than three. Well, maybe it's not quite the same thing, but you get the point!

For a full breakdown of what accounts you need, go to page 103. Just remember that it pays to put the work in up front and set yourself up for far less hassle down the line. Life is complicated enough.

KNOW YOUR CREDIT SCORE

As I always say, your credit score is the only "grade" that matters after you leave high school or college. Most of us know that your credit score is the primary number financial institutions look at when deciding how financially responsible you are. Meaning, it impacts your interest rates and whether you can even take out a line of credit or mortgage at all. Credit scores range from 300 to 850, and ideally you want to keep yours at 760 or above.

Credit agencies are not required to notify you when your credit score goes up or down, so your biggest to-do here is to make sure you're checking yours regularly. Many banks now automatically share your credit score for free, on your monthly statements, but you should still check it proactively. You can find out your numerical score easily on Credit Karma, and you can get your full credit report at AnnualCreditReport.com.

There are three major credit bureaus that calculate your score—Equifax, Experian, and TransUnion—and you're entitled to a free report from each bureau annually. In other words, requesting a report should cost you zero dollars, but you still have to remember to ask for it (that is, set a calendar reminder to do so—see page 119).

If you discover that your score is lower than you'd like (remember, you're aiming to get it into the excellent zone of 760+), don't panic. Improving your score is very possible and comes down to three key things:

1. Never miss a payment. This isn't just about credit card payments. It also includes hospital bills, doctors' bills (that are usually mailed to you), and parking tickets!
2. Maintain your oldest lines of credit. Length of history matters, so don't close your oldest credit card.
3. Don't carry credit card debt. Simply said, do whatever you can to pay your credit card bills *in full* every single month, and do your best to stay far, far away from hitting your credit limit.

On that last point, the founder and CEO of Credit Karma, Ken Lin, agrees. "Don't overextend on your credit card," he advises. "Have enough credit where you're never using more than 20 percent of your credit limit at any point in time, and ideally pay it off each month. It's as simple as that. If you do that—have [a few] credit cards and pay them off each month—you're going to have a great credit score."

CREDIT SCORE MYTH, DEBUNKED

There are lots of myths out there about credit, so let's settle the score (pun intended) once and for all: you will *not* be penalized for checking your credit score frequently. Checking your own score is considered a "soft inquiry." If you apply for a loan or an apartment and a third party checks your score, on the other hand, it's considered a "hard inquiry." If too many of these hard inquiries happen in a short period, it *can* lower your score, but only temporarily.

KNOW YOUR NUMBERS

At this point, you should be able to calculate some quick numbers that will become the foundation for your plan. We're going to start using these numbers in the next chapter and beyond. You'll need the following:

YOUR NET WORTH

Net worth = assets—debts

Your net worth is essentially a total of all the assets you listed in the last step (like savings and retirement accounts), minus any outstanding debt (including unpaid credit card balances). This number gives you a high-level view of your financial state, and it's a great way to track your progress as you go.

YOUR MONTHLY TAKE-HOME PAY

Actual cash that hits your bank account each month after taxes and retirement contributions

This is the money you actually have to work with. Thinking about your earnings in these terms can be a very powerful reset: if your annual salary is $100,000, don't think of it that way. It's more like $67,000 in post-tax dollars, depending on where you live. That's a *big* difference.

This number should also include any additional income you are bringing home from freelancing or other gig work.

This may be highly variable, so see page 71 for how to factor this in without having to calculate it fresh every month.

YOUR CREDIT SCORE
That magic number between 300 and 850
As you just learned, this number helps lenders gauge how financially responsible you are and plays a big role in your ability to buy a home, get a great credit card APR, and more. Ideally, you always keep your score above 760.

BONUS: HOW TO GET FINANCIALLY ORGANIZED WITH SOMEONE ELSE

All of these organizational basics are easy enough to grasp. But what happens when there's someone else in the mix?

When you put money and relationships together, things can get *really* complicated. For the most part, you don't hear an abundance of stories about how much people *love* managing money with their partner. The stories that usually get to me, at least, are about how money is dragging down a relationship. But with a combination of honest conversations and simple technology, I do think smart financial planning and relationship bliss are both possible.

There are three core moves you'll need to make:

1. ALIGN YOUR VALUES

Someone once told me that the most important financial decision you'll ever make is whom you marry (and they didn't mean you should marry someone who has money). They meant that it's critical to marry someone whose financial values align with your own.

At LearnVest, we leveraged the work of a number of financial psychologists to identify the most prevalent values people hold when it comes to money: **stability, luxury, ambition, freedom, generosity, and legacy.**

Set aside time to sit down with your partner and rank them, from most to least important. You can do this now, whether you've been married for a decade or just got engaged. Think about how much each of these values matters to you, and ask your partner to do the same.

Then have an open conversation about both your areas of overlap and the places where you don't see eye to eye. The chances that you will have ranked these in the exact same order are slim, but that's okay. What matters is that you both understand how each of your individual approaches to money impacts your decision making.

This strategy works. Take it from Melanie Whelan, CEO of SoulCycle: "Agree on some parameters up front on what's important to each of you . . . My husband and I value similar things (education, travel, investing in our communities) and talked a lot about that before we married. As our family, resources, and lives have expanded, we always come back to what's most important to us as we make financial decisions."

Daphne Oz, author and TV host, agrees: "Recognize that money is often a surrogate for other conversations. In talking about money, you unearth deep needs around security, love, aspirations for the future. Don't be afraid of these conversations. They help you get to know the one you love that much better."

We all make countless money decisions every day. And when we're in a relationship, a certain amount of compromising needs to take place. The better you understand each other, the easier it will be to navigate these decisions, no matter how big or small.

2. PICK YOUR COMBO METHOD

When you get married, one of the biggest decisions you'll make is how to combine your finances. Will you merge all your individual accounts into a single or several joint accounts? Will you open a joint checking account, while still keeping separate accounts for your savings? There are a lot of different variations to consider, but at their core here are your options:

Option 1: Combine Everything

As the name suggests, in this model your finances are joined 100 percent. On the plus side, this option gives you the fewest number of accounts to manage and helps you streamline. It creates clarity: you'll have a shared set of savings goals and know exactly what you each can put toward discretionary spending. And it builds transparency. Leveraging PFM apps and automated alerts, you'll both have full visibility into everything.

On the flip side, it takes away some privacy. Want to buy your spouse a supersecret birthday present? It's hard to surprise someone with a new flat-screen TV when your funds are 100 percent combined. It's also complicated to untangle your finances, if you ever find yourself in that challenging position.

> **TIP:** People who succeed in a fully combined model tend to agree on a "no-go amount." It's the dollar limit that triggers a conversation. For example, if your "no-go amount" is $500 and you want to buy a plane ticket to Hawaii, it's something you have to discuss with your partner.
>
> Settle on a number that fits with your financial plan. The goal is not to have to run every little purchase by each other but to have conversations about the big stuff. To get in the

habit of doing this, set up auto-alerts on your debit or credit card that trigger an email when you make a purchase over this amount and use an email account that you both can access.

Option 2: Combine Some

In a semi-combined model, you'll combine the majority of your accounts, but you each will have a small savings account that's yours and yours alone. The upside is that it's an inherently equitable system: because it's uncommon for couples to have identical incomes, you can allocate an equal percentage of your paycheck (not an equal number of dollars) to the shared account, and the remaining percentage goes to your personal one. For your shared account, I recommend putting aside at least 75 percent, to cover your joint essentials.

By also keeping a private savings account, each partner still gets full autonomy to spend freely throughout the month—eliminating day-to-day friction while still encouraging healthy discussions about your shared assets and how you're using those to meet your goals.

Jon Stein, founder and CEO of the online advisory platform Betterment, endorses this option, which he calls the "three-pot system." Here's how he describes it: "The 'three-pot system' is a trending solution to help couples get organized. It includes one joint account for shared expenses—like rent, new furniture, and electricity bills—and two separate accounts for each spouse's personal expenses. As things change, you will want to reassess what is paid for from which account; however, this system is a nice way to transition to shared finances and build up that crucial trust."

Option 3: Combine Nothing

The final option is to keep your accounts fully separate. This is not ideal from a financial-planning perspective, because you never have a full picture of how your household is doing. Plus, it introduces tremendous complexity because you have to figure out how to pay for joint bills and expenses. I believe when couples are on the same page about their money, they ultimately have better relationships overall. It encourages you to work toward something together and build your dream life as a unit.

3. LEVERAGE TECHNOLOGY

In many relationships, one partner handles most of the finances. As tempting as this is, getting on the same page about your money requires you to *both* show up and do the work.

Plus, being a team about your money makes it more fun. Jason Brown, founder and CEO of the FinTech start-up Tally, recommends that you "set aside an entire day to discuss where you want to be financially in five years, ten years, twenty years. Go deep, listen hard, and don't judge. Keep going until you've painted a financial picture that legitimately inspires you both. Creating a plan and managing day-to-day money decisions is much easier when you are both excited by a common destination."

A lot of people prefer to bury their heads in the sand about things that are stressful, money included. This has a negative impact for an individual, but it's even worse in a relationship. The best way to protect yourself is simply to stay informed and involved.

Which apps are best for couples? Go to page 184 to see the full rundown, and happy planning!

STEP 2: GET FOCUSED

Now that you know what you have, it's time to craft that information into a budget. In *Financially Fearless*, I broke down an amazing principle called the 50/20/30 method, which I believe is the best way to think about your spending and saving. Let's do a quick recap.

The 50/20/30 numbers represent the three categories into which you should be splitting your take-home pay, the number we calculated on page 62. As a reminder, this is the cash that hits your bank account each month, *after* taxes and *after* retirement contributions. Fifty percent *or less* of it will go to your essentials, 20 percent *or more* to saving for your future, and 30 percent *or less* to your lifestyle. So if your household takes home $10,000 a month after taxes, that's $5,000, $2,000, and $3,000, respectively.

Your budget might not conform exactly to these ratios, but use them as a strong guiding principle as you think about your money.

ESSENTIALS (50 PERCENT)

Your essential dollars are earmarked for the basics. This covers your housing cost (rent or mortgage), utilities, groceries, and transportation to and from work. If you're in a city, that might be your MetroCard; if you're in a suburb, that might be your car payment—plus gas and insurance.

Basically, we're talking everything you need to live and earn an income. Note: if child care is required for you to work, that counts as an essential too.

Remember, 50 percent is the upper limit. All of these expenses should be *less than* 50 percent of your take-home pay.

TIP: Whether we rent or own, our housing costs are one of our largest expenses. I recommend that your housing cost be no more than 30–35 percent of your take-home pay, leaving 15–20 percent for your remaining essentials. Remember that overspending on your home leads to more spending elsewhere, from larger utility bills to more furniture to buy, so if you can get your housing costs down to 25 percent, your finances will feel better everywhere else. And, in case you are tempted to splurge on a bigger house or apartment than you need, remind yourself that for the most part we spend very little of our waking hours in our home.

FUTURE (20 PERCENT)

The next 20 percent of your take-home pay goes toward your future. The things that go in this bucket are the reasons we plan to begin with: to build financial security (read: emergency savings) and save for future purchases.

Where do you see yourself in the next five or ten years? Excuse the job interview question, but it's an important one when it comes to financial planning, because whatever you imagine for yourself, odds are that you'll need money to achieve that vision.

Do you want to buy your first home in a couple of years? Have kids? (Now that I'm on the other side of this, I can confirm that kids practically eat money!) Quit your job and take an adult gap year? It's literally never too early to start saving.

In addition, all monthly payments toward student loans, your Roth IRA, and your child's college savings account (known as a 529 plan) count as part of this bucket.

No matter what you're saving for, you should be putting away *20 percent or more* of your take-home pay. I say "or more," because this is an area where overachieving is encouraged. Remember, as we live longer, there's a new equation for our retirement savings and added pressure on our wallets. The earlier you prepare for the future, the easier it will be to hit that retirement goal.

TIP: Set up separate savings accounts by name to literally see your progress on these goals one by one! Trust me, there's nothing more rewarding than seeing the balance on that "sabbatical fund" grow and grow. There are tons of tools, like Digit, that will help you automate your savings. More on that soon.

LIFESTYLE (30 PERCENT)

Now for the fun part. You work to live the life you want. The last 30 percent of your take-home pay is yours to savor. Whatever matters to you—be it a yoga class twice a week, MLB season tickets, or a weekly date night—these are your funds to play with.

Remember that budgeting is not about deprivation. It's about finding balance between enjoying life in the present and planning for a secure future.

So take that *30 percent (or less)* of your take-home pay and go live your best life.

"BUT WHAT IF . . . ?"

Of course, no two budgets look exactly the same, and as the nature of money and work continues to evolve, new variables seem to pop up all the time—like the introduction of occasional freelance income into a formerly predicable budget.

Let's look at some of the most common questions I get around budgeting.

WHAT IF I GET A BONUS?

If you have a job where your bonus is relatively guaranteed (that is, a certain dollar amount each December), you can treat it like salary and include it in your take-home pay amount. But if your bonus is a sales commission or doled out on the whim of your employer, don't bake it into your budget. The goal here is to set yourself up to live on income that is fully and entirely reliable.

If you receive a one-off bonus or a commission comes through, I recommend the 90/10 rule. What that means is that 90 percent of your bonus goes toward your top financial goal (think of it as an acceleration of your future funds) and 10 percent is yours to enjoy now (think of it like a lifestyle bonus).

HOW DO I BUDGET IF I'M A FREELANCE OR GIG WORKER?

If you're part of the 36 percent of Americans on a freelance career path, it *is* still possible to use 50/20/30. It just requires a look in the rearview mirror. Look at how much you brought home last year, or better yet, the last two or three years if you have the data and it's still relevant (that is, your rate and volume of work are more or less the same), and take the monthly average. If you've been freelancing for a while, use all of the data available to you and take a monthly average over several years. If you don't yet have a track record, it's okay to guess, but be extremely conservative.

Identify what you can reasonably make on a monthly basis and think of this the same way you would your regular paycheck. If you have an amazing month where money rolls in, enjoy the success, but remember to pay it forward. Put that additional income into a savings account, so that you can use it to cover your 20 percent contribution (*not* withdraw for daily expenses) if you have a slower month ahead.

THIS ASSUMES MY EXPENSES ALL HIT ON A MONTHLY BASIS, BUT MY SPENDING COMES IN WAVES. NOW WHAT?

One of the most critical budgeting concepts is non-monthly expenses. These are things that don't happen on a monthly basis, but most definitely will happen: insurance premiums, real estate taxes, holiday shopping, family vacations, you name it. You have to plan not only for these types of expenses (the expected but sporadic) but also for the unexpected ones, like needing to support an aging parent financially or having to pay for another cycle of IVF. Again, look back at your historical data and get a rough ballpark of how much these expenses cost you in a year. Is it $2,000, $20,000?

Take the annual amount, divide by 12, and then you'll know exactly how much to set aside each month so that no non-monthly expense catches you without a cash reserve. The goal here is to avoid ever having to dip into savings.

STEP 3: BASIC FINANCIAL SECURITY

Because I'm a financial planner, lots of people talk to me about how they feel that they should be investing more. It's become part of the zeitgeist, whether we realize it or not (turn on the news for five minutes, and you're likely to hear about the market's performance).

My response? Yes, investing is great, *but* that doesn't mean you should be running out and spending your paycheck on Apple (or any other single company, even if it seems like a "sure thing") stock. Generally speaking, the number one place most people should invest more is in their retirement accounts. I cannot stress this enough. Simply put, saving for retirement *is* investing, and it's a smart and tax-advantaged way to do so. Plus, with technology, it's easier than ever to allocate it and forget it. Once you're maxing out your retirement contributions, we can talk about supplemental investing. More on that soon.

At LearnVest, we often call step 3 of a financial plan the "Monopoly step" because you don't get to pass go until you have your basic financial security in check. This refers to three critical things:

1. You're on track for retirement, making significant, if not the maximum allowable, contributions: for 2019, that's $19,000 in a 401(k) and $6,000 in an IRA.
2. You have no credit card debt, carrying zero balance month to month.
3. You have a full emergency savings account, enough to cover anywhere from three to twelve months of expenses, depending on your personal situation. (More on that shortly.)

These steps to basic financial security are designed to protect you from catastrophe. If you lose your job or have a major financial crisis, I want to make sure you are debt-free and have emergency savings to cushion the blow.

So before you move on to any other financial goal, you have to master these three components. Let's get to it.

RETIREMENT

PSA: America is not on track for retirement. In chapter 2, we talked about how as a society, we're in the process of fundamentally transforming what retirement looks like. We may "use up" some of our retirement years earlier in our careers as sabbaticals, we are likely to live longer, and we may be working, or at least picking up jobs via the gig economy, much longer. All of these variables impact how we need to approach retirement savings. Our earning years have been reshuffled and extended, and our life expectancy has gone up. So for starters, let's stop planning for one single block of work-free time (age sixty-seven and up) and start to think about what we might want—and need—to do for what our "retirement" may actually look like.

If there's one reason to take retirement savings seriously, look no further than what's currently happening with American retirees. A 2018 analysis by *The Wall Street Journal* argued that we're in the midst of a retirement crisis. It found that fifteen million households across the United States—yes, fifteen *million*—that are in or nearing retirement age are not prepared. Specifically, it reported that "more than 40% of households headed by people age 55–70 lack sufficient resources to maintain their living standard in retirement."

Worse yet, the Economic Policy Institute reports that nearly 50 percent of Americans have zero retirement account savings, and a 2018 survey by Empower found that Americans are on track to replace only 64 percent of their income in retirement, significantly below the recommended 80 percent.[1] Plus, Financial Engines found that 25 percent of people do not contribute enough to their 401(k) to take advantage of their full employer match—leaving a sizable bonus on the table.[2]

These stats are troubling. Many of the trends we've talked about have played a role, like the squeeze of supporting kids while also caring for aging parents and our gains in life expectancy. On top of that, the cost of health care has steadily risen, which means that many of these retirees have piles of debt (in a few shapes and sizes—including six times more student loan debt than their peers just over a decade ago).[3]

All of this makes me so worried for America, but I remain hopeful that technology, innovation, and smart planning can help us get to a better spot.

WHERE TO BUILD YOUR RETIREMENT FUNDS

Remember that retirement is your first vehicle for investing. So here are the six major types of retirement accounts and a breakdown of how they work.

	WHAT IT IS	2019 CONTRIBUTION
TRADITIONAL 401(K)	An employer-sponsored account into which you can save money from every paycheck. In retirement, the money you withdraw—including earnings—will be taxed based on whatever income bracket you're in at the time.	$19,000 (or $25,000 if you're age 50+)
ROTH 401(K)	Same as the above, but your contributions are post-tax dollars, meaning that when you withdraw funds in retirement, they will come out tax-free.	$19,000 (or $25,000 if you're age 50+)
403(B)	Operates almost exactly like a 401(k) plan but is usually offered to those who work for public schools and tax-exempt organizations.	$19,000 (or $25,000 if you're age 50+)
TRADITIONAL IRA	An individual retirement account into which you can save money and receive a tax deduction if you meet certain income requirements or if you don't have an employer-sponsored retirement plan—such as a 401(k)—available to you.	$6,000 (or $7,000 if you're age 50+)
ROTH IRA	An individual retirement account into which you can save after-tax money if you meet certain income requirements. In retirement, the money you withdraw—both your deposits and all of your earnings—is entirely tax-free.	$6,000 (or $7,000 if you're age 50+)
NONDEDUCTIBLE IRA	An individual retirement account into which you can save money if you don't meet the income requirements for a traditional IRA and you have an employer-sponsored retirement plan available to you. Your contributions to this plan are not deductible on your taxes, but that also means you won't pay taxes on the money when you withdraw it during retirement. You will, however, pay taxes on any earnings.	$6,000 (or $7,000 if you're age 50+)

Source: *Financially Fearless*

In theory, you can contribute to a patchwork of retirement accounts—the contribution limits apply to each account type. Let's say you have a traditional 401(k) ($19,000) through work and a Roth IRA ($6,000), for example. In that scenario, you could contribute as much as $25,000 to your retirement savings each year. (But you can't put $6,000 in both a traditional IRA *and* $6,000 in a Roth IRA in the same year.)

THE REPLACEMENT RATIO

As a good way to benchmark how much you'll need in your retirement years, use an 80 percent replacement ratio. In other words, assume that you'll want at least 80 percent of your current take-home pay for each year you plan not to work. I don't use 100 percent because we can assume that some current expenses won't be a concern down the line—like mortgage payments and child-care costs.

Most 401(k) providers offer tremendously helpful retirement calculators (generally found on the institution's website) that let you enter in a few custom data points (your age, current salary, life expectancy, and so on) and then spit out a projection for how "on track" you are. Take your new knowledge into account when you think about how many years you plan to work and how many years you're going to plan for.

Your retirement saving goal is going be unique to your situation, but for a *very* general benchmark, Fidelity has proposed a good rule of thumb:

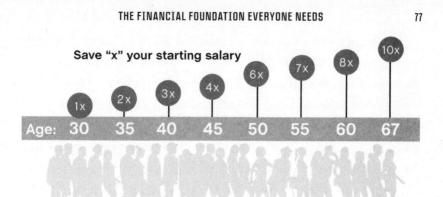

Source: "How Much Do I Need to Save for Retirement?," *Fidelity Viewpoints,* August 21, 2018, www.fidelity.com.

In other words, Fidelity suggests that by age thirty, you should have at least one times your current salary in your retirement account, by age forty you should have three times, and so on. This chart runs you through age sixty-seven, so consider this a baseline plan, and adjust yours depending on your own retirement aspirations.

CREDIT CARD DEBT

Here's the thing about credit card debt: it's actually *designed* to grow. And that's why it can be such a daunting financial hurdle to overcome.

At his company, Tally, Jason Brown is working to help Americans lessen the burden of credit cards. In his own words, "Credit card debt is at a record high of $1 trillion. This means people are flushing billions of dollars in interest and late fees down the toilet. Credit cards are great for their convenience and rewards, but they often come at an unfair price for the majority of consumers."

These billions of dollars in interest will likely mean a tough road ahead for many Americans and their families. As the use of cash has declined (more on that in chapter 7), it's become easier to ramp up our credit card spending and put ourselves into the risky position of credit card debt. Which means the crisis could worsen going forward, if we don't take steps to stop it.

To give you a quick example of how fast credit card debt can grow, the highest annual percentage rate (APR) that you'll see on a savings account in 2018 is around 2 percent, while the average credit card debt accumulates interest at over 16 percent APR.[4] So, $100 in savings is on a path to grow to $102 saved. But $100 of debt quickly becomes $116 owed.

Credit card debt is no joke. Just like losing extra weight, shedding our debt starts by getting extremely motivated.

YOUR PAY-DOWN PLAN

If you carry a balance on multiple cards, your first step is to rank your credit cards from highest to lowest interest rates. It's almost incredible to me that this wasn't always the case, but credit card statements are now legally required to tell you how much interest you're paying.

You'll need to make minimum payments across all cards to protect your credit score, but beyond that get hyper-focused on putting every extra dollar toward paying down your highest interest rate (read: most expensive) card.

Here are other ways to hack your debt pay down:

▷ **CONSIDER AUTOMATED PAY-DOWN TOOLS.** The aforementioned company Tally calls itself an "automated debt manager." Its technology lets you scan in your cards, and then it issues you a line of credit based on your financial picture. Then it uses that money to pay down your balances in the most optimized way possible, minimizing fees and making the right payment to the right card at the right time (you do pay interest on the credit it issues, but it's generally lower than the rates you are paying on your existing debt). Similarly, Digit has introduced Digit Pay, a tool that automates an extra payment on your credit card each month with money it judges that you don't need in your checking account, based on your past spending patterns.

Here's how Brown thinks about tools like Tally: "To overcome credit card debt, we need to be pragmatic. The goal is to get out of debt as fast as possible while minimizing interest and fees along the way. But that requires a lot of time and complicated math. Credit card debt also comes with stress and anxiety, and those emotions can affect our ability to make good decisions. By letting technology do the heavy lifting for us, we can achieve our financial goals and live happier lives."

▷ **MAKE SEMI-BIMONTHLY PAYMENTS.** If you work for a traditional company or employer, your paycheck likely hits twice per month. If you can, make a second credit card payment mid-month too. As if credit card debt weren't expensive enough, interest accrues daily, so by making two payments per month, you'll save a handful of dollars in interest. (Remember, every little bit counts.)

▷ **AVOID SPENDING TRIGGERS.** We all have certain triggers that drive us to spend. Maybe it's driving past your local Target on the way home or getting a "SALE!!" email from your favorite store. Do what you need to in order to avoid these triggers: take a new route home, unsubscribe from the email list, and put your credit card on ice, literally. This is one of my favorite money hacks of all time, and because I share it so often, I can't tell you how many pictures I've gotten over the years from people showing off their freezers, filled with ice cream, frozen pizzas—and credit cards. And if you use mobile pay (that is, Apple Pay, Google Pay, or Samsung Pay), do the digital equivalent of putting your card on ice by going into the app and removing your credit cards for now; you can add them back once your spending freeze is up.

▷ **ENLIST A BUDDY.** Just like with going to the gym, having someone to keep you accountable around your spending never hurts. When you're committed to erasing your debt, tell your friends, tell your family. This is a smart way to enlist them to help you resist temptation when it comes to spending. Think about it this way: your friends never text you asking if you want to make a big credit card payment together on Friday night. Every text you get is someone asking you to do something that comes with a price tag. When your friends know you're trying to save, it helps everyone be more cognizant of where you're coming from. Everyone can get on board with more thoughtful options for socializing, like a potluck instead of a pricey restaurant or a walk outside instead of a gym class.

EMERGENCY SAVINGS

The last part of your basic financial security is your emergency savings. Or as I call it, your freedom fund.

Simply put, a freedom fund is an amount of money in liquid savings—meaning it's available within a second's notice—stashed away to support you in the event of life's inevitable curveballs.

Keep in mind that as an entrepreneur I'm very comfortable with taking risks. I was born a risk taker and will always be one. But the reason I'm so comfortable with risk is that I make sure to always have a safety net. Having a freedom fund gives me the freedom to take chances without worrying that I could be endangering the financial health of my family.

WHY IT'S NOT OPTIONAL

When I work with people on their financial plans, many are adamant about why they *don't* need an emergency fund. They tell me they're super responsible financially, they have some money in savings, their expenses are consistent from month to month.

Those are all great things, but I've watched enough people go through crises of all types to tell you that no matter how well you might be doing, if/when disaster strikes, you're going to wish you had something to fall back on. As I said in the introduction, I lost my dad when I was fourteen years old. Luckily, my family had emergency savings, which allowed my mother, who had three kids and a full-time job as a nurse practitioner, to take a number of months off from working so that she could be there for us kids emotionally and manage the gut-wrenching transition our family had to make.

When you're going through life's biggest challenges, I *never* want your finances to limit your choices. Money won't make all your problems go away, but a good financial plan will give you as many options for dealing with them as possible.

HOW MUCH DO YOU NEED?

Calculating your target freedom fund amount is simple, because you've already done the legwork. Hark back to your 50/20/30 budget. Remember that your "50" is the bare minimum required to live your life. This includes only the expenses that are urgently necessary, like your grocery bill, mortgage payment, or day care.

To figure out how much you should have in your freedom fund, take the number you calculated as your "50," and multiply it by 3, 6, 9, or 12, depending on the following:

MULTIPLY BY 3	if you have no major financial obligations and make under $100,000 annually. If you're young, not yet married, and do not own a home, you likely fit into this group. So let's say your simplified monthly living expense is $3,000. You'll need a freedom fund of at least $9,000 that you leave untouched.
MULTIPLY BY 6	if your financial life is more complicated: if you're married or partnered with both people working and have one or more big financial obligations (like a mortgage).
MULTIPLY BY 9	if you make over $100,000. Why should someone who makes more need more of a safety net? Here's the kicker: when you make more money, it's harder to find a new job at the same level. And by the same token, the more advanced you are in your career, the longer it generally takes to secure a new role on that career trajectory should you get laid off or quit. There are simply fewer of those jobs out there. That's why your freedom fund should include nine months of living expenses to carry you through a potentially long job hunt.
MULTIPLY BY 12	if you have children and/or are supporting an aging parent. Because I like to play it safe when family is involved, I recommend stashing away an entire year's worth of expenses. I know that's a lot, but if you're in this bucket, there are more people in your household who could be affected.

Remember, this cash is for *true emergencies only*. Not a trip you want to take or a kitchen upgrade. It's for fixing the broken-down car you need to drive to work, paying the bills during a period when you are out of work, caring for a sick family member—you get the picture.

STEP 4: BUILD YOUR FUTURE

Of all the steps, this one is my favorite and definitely the most fun. It's the one where you get to dream about what your future life will look like.

Think about how you approach most of the things you want to accomplish in life. Want to train for a marathon? You build out a training plan. Want to lose ten pounds? You come up with an exercise and diet regimen. Want to be promoted at work? You outline your recent achievements and map out your career goals.

So why *wouldn't* you use the same planning muscle for your financial goals? The good news is that it's actually super easy; it's just basic math.

To figure out how much you need to save each month to reach a specific goal, you simply set a target date, then divide how much you need to have saved by how many months you have to save it.

Let's say you want to buy a home that requires a $100,000 down payment in two years, and you already have $50,000 saved. How much do you need to save per month, given that you have twenty-four months to do it? About $2,000 (or $2,083.33) to be exact—not including interest. Or if you want to take that adult gap year on your fortieth birthday in three years, and you'll need $30,000 to do it, you'll have to put aside just over $800 each month.

All too often, we have a tendency to approach saving for the future by simply putting whatever is left over after bills have been paid toward our goals. There's a better way!

Whatever your goals may be, you want to be proactive and intentional about saving for them. That's why the "20" of your 50/20/30 budget comes before the "30"; I want you to put your future before your present. To help you stay organized and efficient, here are some tips:

▷ **KEEP THINGS SEPARATE.** For any specific goal (or goals) you're saving for, set up a separate account or a sub-account. That way, when you log in to your financial provider of choice, you're in a position to clearly see how you're tracking. If you keep *all* of your savings in one giant pot, the total balance may look higher, but the motivation—and the rush from seeing your progress—will be lacking.

▷ **AUTOMATE.** I'll get into automation in much more detail in chapter 6, but for now just know that this is definitely a place to kick into autopilot. You'll know how much you'll need each month to hit your goal, so all you have to do is set up a direct savings contribution to transfer automatically as soon as your paycheck hits. Out of sight, out of mind.

▷ **STAY FLEXIBLE.** Most of us have a finite amount of resources to work with every month. There are only two ways to change that equation: you can earn more or spend less. Want to get to a goal faster? Cut down on your "30" spending and funnel more into your "20."

▷ **TRAIN YOUR MIND.** Sometimes, hacking your wallet may require some hacking of your personal psychology to help you stay motivated. When I'm focused on accomplishing something, there are a few ways I push myself. I love productivity apps, which help me ensure I'm spending my time (another limited resource) in the direction of my goal. And I'm addicted to countdown apps. I pick a date that I'm excited about and check in all the time as I get closer. I'm also not above a good Post-it on the mirror, and I'm guilty of having a note on my phone called "fun," where I track all the fun trips, events, or purchases I'm working toward. I know, that sounds simple and perhaps even a little silly, but it's how I stay excited when I'm focused on a goal.

STEP 5: PROTECT YOURSELF

Insurance is critical. Simply put, insurance is there to protect you from the horrific curveballs that could devastate your financial life. In a perfect world, "Protect Yourself" would be the first step. But that's not how human psychology works. It's so much easier—and more enjoyable—to think about goals that excite us (that is, our dreams) than to try to wrap our heads around preparing for the worst (that is, our fears). As a result, too many people end up avoiding this topic entirely.

My lifelong mentor, Ann Kaplan, once said to me, "Imagine if I could promise you'd never go bankrupt? Simply get the right insurance at all times." Insurance protects you from fundamental financial demise. From there, I got it. Always have the appropriate insurance for your life's needs.

Because none of us *want* to go underwater with our finances, being properly insured protects against just that. I know insurance isn't sexy, but it's critical to every financial plan. So, if there's one section of this chapter to pay close attention to, it's right here.

The first step is understanding what types of insurance you need. For each type, ask yourself: (1) Does this apply to me? (If you don't own a home, for example, you don't need homeowner's insurance.) (2) Do I have the right policy? (3) Do I have enough coverage?

KEY TYPES OF INSURANCE

Health	Disability
Auto	Life insurance
Homeowner's	Long-term care
Renter's	Umbrella

Our insurance needs are constantly evolving. It's up to you to make sure your policies stay up-to-date, no matter what happens. So let's take a closer look at the critical types of insurance you may need.

HEALTH

In today's political climate, there is still uncertainty around whether every individual will be legally required to have health care in the United States—or face penalties—under the "individual mandate clause" of the Affordable Care Act.

Legality aside, I believe everyone should have health insurance, period. With the cost of health care being as high as it is, this is not a place where anyone should take risks. Without insurance, a single hospital visit can place tremendous strain on our wallets, and even send us spiraling into debt. In fact, the Consumer Financial Protection Bureau found that medical bills are the number one reason that debt collectors chase people down.[5] Nobody chooses to be ill or injured, but we can take steps not to let illness or injury derail our finances.

When it comes to health insurance, make sure not only that you have it—100 percent of the time, especially in between jobs—but also that your emergency savings are sufficient to cover your highest deductible.

There are a number of companies working to make health insurance more affordable, like Oscar Health and Clover Health. These are particularly worth looking into if you don't have an employer-sponsored plan available to you.

Our health is our most valuable asset. We only have one body, and we need it to serve us well!

AUTO

If you own a car, auto insurance is a legal requirement. Focus here on ways to cut down on your auto insurance bill. If you have an emergency savings account, you might consider raising your deductible, and if you have a pristine driving record, that can earn you a discount up to 10 percent.

If you use a car-share service, be sure to read the fine print and understand how much liability coverage is included in your agreement. Depending on the plan, you may choose to supplement with non-owner car insurance.

HOMEOWNER'S

If you own a home, this is another must, primarily because most lenders require proof of insurance before giving you a mortgage. In addition to the basics, make sure to consider what unique risks your home faces (are you in a flood zone or an area prone to earthquakes, for example?).

You can create flexibility in your monthly premiums by raising your deductible—a move you should consider making only if you have enough savings to cover your out-of-pocket costs should a claim happen.

RENTER'S

If you're renting a home, this is crucial. There are a whole slew of start-ups out there using modern technology to make this incredibly quick and easy to purchase, like Lemonade or Jetty. You can get a renter's policy nearly instantly, and the average cost is under $16 a month.[6]

I cannot tell you how many times I've heard from people that renter's insurance has saved them from financial catastrophe. In the early days of LearnVest, all new employees got a financial plan, and one employee wisely decided to purchase renter's insurance as a result. Two weeks later, a fire sprang up from the pizza shop she lived above, and her apartment suffered serious damage.

Luckily, even though she had only paid a month's worth of her new insurance plan, the policy covered the cost of new furniture, new clothing, and new computers and helped with the (considerable) cost of the hotel she had to stay at in the fire's aftermath. This is just one small example of how a simple precautionary measure can make a measurable impact.

DISABILITY

Disability insurance is designed to protect your income if something happens that renders you physically unable to work. It comes in a few shapes and sizes. You'll need to consider both short- and long-term plans and also decide between "own occupation" and "any occupation" plans. Own occupation means that you'll be covered if you're not able to perform your *own* specific job, whereas "any" kicks in only if you're not able to perform *any* job.

If you're employed full-time, disability insurance is often available through your employer. If your employer pays for disability coverage on your behalf, make sure that you have enough coverage to make up for your lost income, and if not, consider taking on more at your own cost. Often people need to supplement what their employers offer them.

LIFE INSURANCE

The goal of life insurance is to cover your financial obligations in the event something tragic happens. It's awful to even think about, but it's critical for protecting your family. It's especially important if your income currently supports your spouse, if you have children, if you're supporting extended family members, and if you have large debts (like student loans or a mortgage).

As with other types of insurance, you'll have to make a lot of choices here. You can decide between a term policy (which will cover you for a set amount of years) and a whole policy (which will stay active for the entirety of your life and often has flexibility in how you can access the cash in the policy). I recommend talking to an expert to decide which type of life insurance is best for your unique situation. Get a free opinion or two from a high-quality adviser, and then consider both recommendations.

If some amount of life insurance is offered through your employer, typically that is a good, inexpensive option, but know that it rarely covers what you would need in total. So, ask your HR leader to explain exactly how that works. Oftentimes opting in for that coverage makes a ton of sense. And finally, if your needs are relatively simple, check out Ethos, Ladder, or Fabric—three FinTech start-ups working to make life insurance cheaper, easier, and less intimidating for all of us.

LONG-TERM CARE

As we discussed in chapter 2, the cost of elder care is incredibly daunting. Long-term-care policies help offset these costs. If you're young, it might be unimaginable to think you might ever need a caregiver or live in a nursing home. But the younger you are when you buy long-term care coverage, the lower rates will be. For example, the initial premium for long-term-care insurance is 8–10 percent lower at age sixty-four than at age sixty-five.[7]

If you're married, you might consider a "shared care" rider, which allows you to share the insurance benefits with your partner. This helps couples maximize their benefits and accounts for the fact that you may need different levels of care.

UMBRELLA

If you have lots of assets that need protecting, an umbrella policy can help give you some extra liability coverage. True to their name, umbrella policies essentially sit on top of your other policies—like auto and homeowner's—to give you extra peace of mind.

HOW TECHNOLOGY HELPS

If analyzing your policies and buying the coverage you need is overwhelming, the good news is that a whole host of technologies are working to improve the insurance experience. This is one area where the FinTech industry—and a new segment called InsureTech—is really shining. Spencer Lazar, a partner at the venture capital firm General Catalyst, which has backed a number of FinTech start-ups, says it best: technology has the "ability to simplify what can otherwise be complicated and overwhelming financial products."

Lemonade, for example, is a forward-thinking new insurance carrier that's not only disrupting all the traditional models of the insurance industry; it's also using artificial intelligence to personalize and tailor each customer's plan to his or her individual needs. Interestingly, the co-founder Daniel Schreiber attributes these innovations to lack of industry knowledge: "[We] knew nothing about insurance when we set out to create Lemonade, and that enabled us (forced us!) to resort to first-principles thinking. The upshot is insurance you can buy in seconds, that pays claims instantly, and that gives back underwriting profits to nonprofits. I think banking, lending, and other areas of finance could be transformed by outsiders applying socially impactful, customer-centric, and technology-first design principles."

There are so many other InsureTech companies out there, and more are popping up all the time. All of which makes me confident the future of insurance will continue to be more seamless, painless, and affordable for everybody.

ESTATE PLANNING

I know—just the title of this section probably makes you want to skip the rest of this chapter and move on. (Please don't, I promise to keep it short and sweet!)

We all know that wills are important (I hope!), but protecting your assets after you are gone goes beyond just having a solid will in place. Whom will you want to make your health decisions if you can't? Whom will you want to be the guardian of your child? Who will carry out your wishes when it comes to supporting a family member in need? These are big, scary, daunting questions. But look at it this way: thinking about them now will give you the peace of mind of knowing that the people you love will be protected in the event that the unthinkable happens.

So don't think twice here. Despite how it sounds, estate planning is *not* just for the 1 percent. I recommend LegalZoom as a good, inexpensive place to start on everything from your living will to power of attorney. Do your research, make these decisions, and sleep better knowing that your family—and your wishes—are fully protected.

STEP 6: INVEST

As you learned in step 3, your retirement account should be your number one investing priority. So if you haven't yet started setting aside your retirement contributions, pause, turn to page 73, and then come back to this chapter.

If you find personal finance confusing, investing is probably the biggest problem area. Don't feel bad. Most books and articles on the topic are full of jargon, designed to be hard for people to understand.

This section won't teach you how to "get rich quick," and it won't give you any tips for "beating the market." But it will run through a few basic rules of thumb that will empower you to make thoughtful, educated investing decisions.

THE RULE OF FIVE

Do you need your money for a goal that's coming up in the next five years? It should not be majorly invested in the stock market.

Why? Over the long term, the market moves in the right direction—up—having made an average of about 10 percent per year over the past hundred years. But in the short term, it has its ups and downs.[8] I don't want you to be in a position of having to cash out when it's in a slump.

At a very basic level, you should follow the rule of five: only invest money in the stock market if you are sure you won't need those funds for five years or longer, to ensure the long-term gains exceed any temporary losses.

LOOK FOR LOW-COST

There are a few different ways you can invest in the stock market. The most common are individual stocks, exchange-traded funds (ETFs), index funds, and mutual funds. Generally speaking, I tend to prefer ETFs and index funds.

Why? ETFs and index funds contain a broad range of stocks. In other words, they have diversification built in; instead of betting on just one company, you're spreading the risk across lots of companies.

Mutual funds have a similar level of diversification, but they tend to have a management fee associated with having an asset manager decide which stocks to include. That might sound like something worth paying for, but in general managed funds do not typically outperform ETFs and index funds.

FIND AN EXPERT

If you know what money you have to invest, what your goals are, and the basics of investing, a trusted financial adviser can be a good resource. When I say trusted, I mean true licensed experts, with designations like CFP®, which stands for Certified Financial Planner™. I think of CFP®s as doctors of money. Becoming a CFP® is a lengthy and rigorous process, and CFP®s are also held to high ethical and professional standards. Try websites like the Garrett Planning Network or your financial institution to find a CFP® you can consult, whether for general investing advice or guidance on specific decisions.

STEP 7: REFRESH

We live at a time when the world around us is changing faster than ever. And if you think back to the trends of chapter 2, our lives are changing right along with it, in a multitude of ways that affect our money. Perhaps you decide to quit your 9–5 to go freelance, or start a family, or go on an around-the-world travel adventure. If you're in your twenties, you're going through what the psychologist Meg Jay deemed "the defining decade." Chances are you're making big choices—about where you live, what you do, and whom you're with—that can have a major impact on your finances. In your thirties, you may be focused on starting or growing a family, and that might mean making some big changes around where you live and work. And in your forties and beyond, you may begin to reevaluate some of those earlier choices; maybe you fall in love with a city that you decide to call home, or maybe you decide to pick up and move across the country. Maybe you finally settle into the career path of your dreams, or maybe you go back to school or transition into an entirely new field.

The point is that when we make these kinds of big, lifestyle-altering decisions—at any age—we should also be reevaluating and adjusting our financial plan to account for them. It should be no surprise that my financial plan back when I was a twentysomething entrepreneur with a then boyfriend (now husband) looks *very* different from our financial plan as a family of four today.

Liana Douillet Guzmán, COO of the tech platform Blockchain, says that her best money tip is "taking an annual review of my financial health, including credit card bills, insurance premiums, FSA accounts, etc. It can feel overwhelming, but it's amazing how many forgotten recurring (and unnecessary) payments and other opportunities for savings I find."

I couldn't agree more, which is why I recommend scheduling a yearly assessment of your plan each and every January. I have this on my calendar, and each year my husband and I sit down to look at (a) whether there have been any big changes to our lifestyle over the past year that we need to account for and (b) whether there might be any changes over the next year that we need to actively plan for.

But this yearly check-in should be the bare minimum; whenever something big happens in your life, it's time to go right back through steps 1–6 of your financial plan. Stepping back and looking at your plan with fresh eyes is an opportunity to think holistically about what you're doing. Here are some of the common life events that might necessitate a refresh of your financial plan:

▷ Change in Relationship Status (for example, moving in together, engagement, marriage)
▷ Career Move (for example, new job, new business, promotion)
▷ New Home (for instance, move, first mortgage, vacation home)
▷ Expanding Family (for example, new baby, pet adoption, aging parents)
▷ New City (for instance, cross-country move)

CHAPTER 4

MAINTAIN GOOD MONEY HABITS

I always like to tell people that money is math. But it's also habits. One of the most important things you can do for your money is live with great money habits 365 days per year. The good news about habits is that you can build them throughout your life. If you're not in good shape today, building a new habit comes down to time and repetition. Here's how to build and maintain good money habits.

KNOW HOW HABITS ARE FORMED

In his book *The Power of Habit*, Charles Duhigg explains that habits go through a cue-routine-reward loop. First, something cues or triggers us to take an action. We go through the routine of that action, and we get a reward.

To use an example from *Financially Fearless*, let's say you have a habit of spending $5 on a snack every day at 4:00 p.m. You have to take a step back and understand what your cue is. Are you hungry at that time? In need of a break from work?

If the real reward is getting some fresh air, maybe you create a new routine of taking a walk around the block instead. Breaking or maintaining any habit starts with understanding this simple psychology.

Creating a new habit starts with identifying a cue. What will your trigger be? You might choose a time (every Friday morning) or link it to another activity (every time you get your paycheck). Next, choose a reward that you'll get after achieving the behavior. This could be everything from treating yourself to a coffee, to sleeping in an extra hour on the weekend. Last, create a plan to put these steps together.

Duhigg recommends that you actually write out your plan: "When [cue], I will [routine], because it provides me with [reward]." Once you put this new cue-routine-reward loop into action, it's only a matter of time before this habit becomes automatic.[1]

SCHEDULE REGULAR CHECKUPS

Recognize that taking care of your money is not a one-and-done game. It requires active maintenance throughout the year.

Forming or revisiting your financial plan is just like going to the doctor for a checkup. It can be a hassle, but as they say, an ounce of prevention is worth a pound of cure. So be proactive and set yourself on a good path for the year ahead! I currently talk to our financial planner at least once a month. Oftentimes it's hard to fit in, but we make it a priority.

In addition to using calendar reminders and a separate email account, make sure to turn on notifications for the money apps you regularly use. Many of them are designed to help you form better money habits, so their product features include helpful nudges reminding you to take actions or useful flags to alert you when something out of the ordinary happens.

Aim to check in on your finances (that is, assets, debts, expenses, and credit score) actively, just as you would if you ran a business. *At the bare minimum*, check all of your financial statements monthly. For those type A overachievers out there, I recommend taking a "money minute" every single day. It's a quick daily gut check that will keep you on track and give you the peace of mind of knowing that everything is under control. Use this time to do a quick scan of whatever personal financial management app you're using. Make sure there are no fraudulent transactions, that any auto-payments or contributions have gone through, that transaction amounts are correct, and that your account balances are where they should be.

CREATE ANTI-GOALS

The behavioral economist Dan Ariely has talked about the idea of setting anti-goals. When you spend on something, you need to understand the trade-off you're making. Daniel Schreiber, CEO of the insurance start-up Lemonade, explains, "When thinking 'Should I spend $100 on this gizmo?' it's important to have something tangible—an anti-goal—that you will *not* get as a result. Then you can feel the emotional pull in a healthy way and truly calculate the value to you of what you're about to spend." In short, this is a simple way to gut check: do you really need it?

RIDE THE DOPAMINE HIGH

You know how it's easier to motivate yourself to get on the treadmill when it's in the next room than it is to schlep to the gym? Countless studies show that even the smallest tweaks in our environment can have a huge impact on our behavior. So try making your money setup so easy to access you don't even have to think about it. A simple trick: keep your personal finance apps right next to the social media apps you *know* you'll check on a regular basis.

Get that dopamine high from Instagram, and then use it to power you through your money minute.

ENLIST CALENDAR ALERTS

In order to stay on track throughout the year, it's time to automate those reminders. Put key to-dos on your digital calendar and set alerts to nudge you when the time comes. It may take a few minutes to set up, but it's a time investment sure to pay off. Think about it this way, would you rather store all these various dates in your brain or in the cloud?

PRO TIP: Set the alerts for a time of day when you're likely to see them right away and have the time and bandwidth to take care of them, like during your lunch hour, or whenever you usually sit down to check personal emails.

KEEP IT SIMPLE

Ryan Alfred, the CEO of Framework Inc., offers a brilliant rule to live by: "I like to keep it simple. Save until it hurts, have a plan, and avoid fees."

I'm all for anything that helps me simplify and save. And I know I'm not alone. "I use a plastic wallet (the Jimi for the curious) that I am fairly sure is designed for children," says Michael Norton, Harvard Business School professor and co-author of *Happy Money*. "But the secret is that unlike leather wallets, it can't expand, so it keeps me from cluttering my wallet—and life—with every possible membership card that exists."

Modern life is complicated enough. We owe it to ourselves to simplify wherever we can.

III

HACK YOUR WALLET

When you see "money" and "hack" in the same sentence, you likely go running to your bank account to make sure every dollar is still there. This section isn't about financial security (but we will get to that, so stay tuned); it's about how to "hack" your wallet in the true tech meaning of the word. It's all about how to automate, optimize, and maximize your money—using a few of the most effective tricks I've learned along the way.

I have a hunch you picked up this book because you want to know how to get more out of your wallet. I'm right there with you. I'm a wife, mom, daughter, sister, friend, and executive, and my life can get pretty crazy. But technology has saved me countless hours (and headaches) around my money, and I want to pass on these tools to you too.

It's time to take action here. My promise is that these small tweaks to how you manage your money can have an outsized impact. New FinTech innovation is happening every day, so consider these straightforward tips just the start of what's possible. Let's go build your financially forward foundation.

CHAPTER 5

HACK 1 //
ONLY HAVE THE ACCOUNTS YOU NEED

In the "Get a Plan" section, you got digitally organized. You went to
work uncovering all of your accounts, linked them to a personal financial management app, and took stock of your numbers, from your net
worth to your credit score to your budget.

If you're like most people, you might have been a bit overwhelmed
by all of the accounts in your name. There's the department store credit
card from your college days or the 401(k) from three jobs ago. There
are two checking accounts—one that had an ATM convenient to your
old home and your new one that lets you use ATMs anywhere. The list
goes on. How are you supposed to stay on top of everything?

Luckily, there is a better way. Far easier, and more effective, is to
simply rein in the number of accounts you have and where you have
them. Fifty percent of Americans have accounts at multiple banks, but
we can do better.[1]

In this chapter, we'll make sure you have the accounts you need—
and only those. We'll also make sure that the accounts you keep are the
best possible ones out there. Essentially, they need to be digital, free

from fees, and set up to help your money grow. Ideally, you'll limit the number of banks and financial institutions you work with to a couple.

Your accounts need to be easy to access as stand-alone accounts, and they have to connect well to your other accounts, too, making it easy to move money around as your financial plan dictates.

At a high level, here's how to set up your account ecosystem. These are the accounts I think everyone needs and how to think about structuring them. (Note: you might need fewer, but certainly not more!)

FINANCIAL INSTITUTION 1			
Checking	Savings	Credit Card	Brokerage

FINANCIAL INSTITUTION 2	
Credit Card	Retirement Accounts

Take a moment to think about your current account ecosystem. If it's not as streamlined, use the following guidelines to help you understand which accounts to keep and which accounts you might want to move elsewhere.

If you don't have a quantity problem, it's time to zero in on quality. When your accounts aren't fitting the bill, it may be time to make a change.

What to look for:

CHECKING

Your go-to spot for money that you spend on a day-to-day basis.

☐ **ONLINE ACCESS.**
This account should be easily accessible online, which means a great user experience every time you log in on desktop and especially on mobile.

☐ **NO-FEE ATMS.**

Who wants to pay to use their own money? In a perfect world, your checking account would have a physical ATM location close to your home.

☐ **NO MAINTENANCE FEES.**

Again, you don't want to pay someone for the honor of holding on to your money. There are many good options that won't charge fees!

SAVINGS

This is where you'll keep everything from your freedom fund to contributions for your next vacation.

☐ **BEST INTEREST RATE.**

The average interest rate hovers around 2 percent as of 2018. This is lower than the average investment market return, but if you're saving for a goal that will hit within five years, this is the safest spot for your money. Online-only banks also tend to pay higher interest rates, which is good in this instance! Newer institutions like Ally Bank, for example, may offer double the interest rate of a traditional bank.[2]

☐ **ABILITY TO CREATE SUB-ACCOUNTS.**

This allows you to easily delineate how your savings line up to each of your goals.

☐ **SAME BANK AS YOUR CHECKING.**

Given how low the interest rate on a checking account is, the goal is not to keep money sitting there. You want to funnel as much money toward your goals as possible. Keeping these accounts within the same bank makes reviewing balances easy, along with instantly transferring funds from checking into savings (we like to avoid the opposite direction!).

WHAT DOES IT MEAN TO BE FDIC INSURED?

You might have heard the term "FDIC insured" before. Essentially, FDIC stands for "Federal Deposit Insurance Corporation." It's a government agency that was established in the Banking Act of 1933, and it's still relevant almost a hundred years later, because it ensures that up to $250,000 (per person, per bank, per account type) is backed by the U.S. government. Before the law was established, it wasn't uncommon for a bank to fail, meaning that your life savings could disappear in an instant. Today—with the exception of a highly extreme situation—we don't have to worry that our bank account balances are in jeopardy.

CREDIT CARDS

I'm not the type of financial planner to tell you that credit cards are a trap. I think they're an easy way to monitor your spending, and they come with a wide range of perks. I *do* think it's a mistake to have so many credit cards that you can't keep track of them. How will you know if you've maxed one out, or that the account has been compromised, if you forget it even exists?!

With the right credit card rewards in place, it's as if your whole life were on sale, with an opportunity to earn airline miles, gift cards, or just plain cash.

Picking out a credit card used to mean going to your local bank and signing up for whatever it had available, most likely the promotion du jour. Now you have all the information you could ever need—and more—to compare the various deals, right at your fingertips.

Start on sites like Credit Karma and NerdWallet. Here's what to look out for:

☐ FEE STRUCTURE.

I want you to be in a position where you can pay your credit card off in full every month. If that's the case, you can worry less about the APR (the interest rate you're charged for carrying a balance) and instead focus in on avoiding any additional fees: annual card fees (this tends to go up as rewards programs are more enticing), inactivity fees (if you don't use the card regularly), balance transfer fees (if you're looking to transfer debt to a card with an introductory 0 percent APR). Note: while many rewards cards charge an annual fee, they may counter that with a guaranteed statement credit if you spend a certain amount or in certain categories. For example, the Chase Sapphire Reserve® has a $450 fee, but offers a $300 credit for any travel-related expenses. If the perks are valuable enough to you, the annual fee may become negligible.

☐ ONLINE ACCESS.

This account should be easily accessible online, which means a great user experience every time you log in on desktop or mobile. Specifically, ensure that the card's online system allows you to easily decode your transactions, schedule payments, and dispute instances of fraud.

☐ INTERNATIONAL EASE OF USE.

In our global world, international fees can get pricey, quick. So if you're someone who likes to travel internationally, make sure your card is equipped to travel with you. Many cards waive these fees as a standard practice, so make sure to choose one of these.

☐ CASH-BACK RESTRICTIONS.

If your card comes with cash-back rewards (which I highly recommend!), read the fine print. Will you get a fixed percentage off all purchases? Are the cash-back rewards capped at a certain number? And do you get a higher percentage back in certain spending categories, like travel or groceries? Take your lifestyle into account here, and do a quick scan of your past spending to see where you'll get the most bang for your buck.

☐ PROMOTIONAL DEALS.

Many rewards cards run generous promos: "100K points for signing up!" "2 round-trip flights!" "$500 credit!" There's a fine balance here—and a whole industry of those trying to maximize the system (you may be familiar with the Points Guy). What I will say is to look for opportunities to maximize your upside, but don't choose a card *only* for the intro offer, only to realize it's not your best long-term option.

☐ LIKELIHOOD OF APPROVAL.

Here's an instance where the internet gives us access to *so* much more info than ever before. Credit Karma will actually tell you how likely it is for someone with your credit score, income, and so on to be approved for any given card before you apply. Why does that matter? When you apply for a card, it triggers a hard inquiry into your credit score—the type of inquiry that can ding your score in the short term. Applying for a card is not a big deal, but if you go on an application spree and find yourself getting rejected along the way, it does have a negative impact. Make sure that you're choosing cards that are realistic for your current financial spot, and as your financial picture improves, continue to evaluate whether you have the best card.

☐ OPTIONS AT YOUR PRIMARY BANK.

This whole section is about "less is more." If the financial institution where you already have an account offers a great credit card that meets your requirements, it will be even easier to log in and manage payments. On the flip side, don't miss out on the perfect fee-free, cash-back rewards card just because it's offered by a different bank. My recommended setup gives you room to log in to two financial institutions, so think about using that wiggle room if needed.

HOW TO CANCEL A CREDIT CARD

If you already have more cards than you can count, or if it's time to switch to a better card, you may need to cancel some existing accounts. While it's important to streamline, you must do so strategically. Closing down lines of credit can negatively impact your credit score. Why? It lowers your available credit, and that's one of the big factors lenders look at.

There are two best practices here:

1. Never close your oldest card. Remember that the length of your credit history matters. Even if your first card is a department store card you've outgrown, make small regular purchases on it to keep it active.

2. Close only one card per year. Cancel the worst offender first (likely the one that's impossible to access digitally or has the highest interest rate). Put all the others you want to cancel in a safe spot and set a calendar reminder annually to knock them off the list, one by one.

BROKERAGE

Outside your checking, savings, and credit card, the other types of accounts you'll need are investment accounts. These come in many shapes and sizes, but the core idea is that they'll help you to maximize your dollars. Checking accounts barely accrue interest, savings accounts accrue interest more slowly than inflation, and credit cards charge you interest! So we're left with our investments to help us get ahead.

So if you're on track for retirement, and you're investing for a goal with a five-year-plus time horizon, it's time for a brokerage account. A growing number of companies fall into this category, giving you more options than ever. You'll find the full list on page 187, but do your homework when it comes to fees and investment options. Here's what to look out for:

☐ **MENU OF INVESTMENT OPTIONS.**

Variety is your friend here. Look for accounts that give you tons of choice when it comes to where your money goes. Are there low-cost ETFs? Do the fund options fit your personal plan, like a target-date fund or a fund that's aligned with your values? Yes, socially responsible ETFs, like environmentally focused funds, are a thing!

☐ **HIGH-TECH.**

Again, we're looking for ease of access and ease of use. Does the account come with a stellar app, so you can see how your money is growing? Many financial institutions have invested in better consumer tech, so make sure you're leveraging the latest developments.

☐ **ACCOUNT MINIMUMS.**

Some investment accounts require a minimum amount to even open an account. Once you know how much you have to start with, ensure that your account of choice will accommodate that number.

☐ **LOW FEES.**

In addition to making sure there are low-fee investment options, do some digging into the actual account fees, which can include annual fees, trading fees, and management fees. You can find most of this info online (there's typically a summary page of account fees), but if you're confused, don't be afraid to pick up the phone and ask.

☐ COMMISSIONS.

For the most part, you may choose to automate most of your investments through target-date funds. Whatever your investment strategy, keep a close eye on how the financial institutions handle commissions. In most cases, you'll be charged every time you buy or sell, but some fees are of course higher than others. Current averages hover around $4.95 per transaction.[3]

RETIREMENT ACCOUNTS

As we talked about in chapter 3, the most important place for you to invest first is in your retirement account. Depending on your work situation, you'll have less flexibility about where your retirement accounts live. For non-work-sponsored accounts, like an IRA, refer to the brokerage checklist. All of the same considerations apply.

That said, there are some specific quirks to consider with 401(k)s, which you'll likely have access to if you're working that 9–5 life. A 401(k) can be a powerful vehicle for growing your money, but only if you take the time to set it up properly. You don't have as much control here as you do with your other accounts, because your company will be the one to pick your plan administrator (ex: Vanguard) and will define the menu of investment options. But there are still things you need to look out for:

☐ EMPLOYER MATCH.

If your company offers to match retirement contributions, this is an absolute no-brainer. First, understand exactly what your company offers, and then make sure you're contributing enough to take full advantage. Note that matches are sometimes on a vesting schedule, which means you have to stay with the company for a certain period of time in order to actually redeem your match dollars. Read the fine print here so that you never leave money on the table.

☐ AUTO-ENROLLMENT.

Many companies now auto-enroll employees into their 401(k)s. According to a 2018 survey from Willis Towers Watson, 73 percent of companies auto-enroll employees (up from 52 percent in 2009).[4] This isn't meant to be sneaky, but rather to encourage employees to start saving for retirement, given that a lack of retirement savings is such a national stressor. Companies—60 percent according to the survey—are also leveraging an auto-escalate feature, which increases your contribution amount gradually over time. Double-check that you're enrolled at the level you want to be—that is, the highest possible amount that fits into your 50/20/30 plan.

YOUR ACTION ITEMS

☐ **IDENTIFY** how many accounts you have and how many financial institutions you're currently using.

☐ **DO** an account audit to make sure that every single one meets the criteria for a best-in-class account.

☐ **CLOSE** accounts as needed—rolling funds into the right spots or slowly phasing out extra credit cards (one per year ideally), depending on the situation.

☐ **SET UP** digital access to all of your remaining accounts. Remember, part of why you picked them is their A-plus digital experience, so take advantage.

CHAPTER 6

HACK 2 //
AUTOMATE EVERYTHING

You did the hard work of building out your financial plan, but sticking to it is a whole other story. It's time to automate your financial life and essentially build a customized algorithm to funnel your dollars to the right spots.

Remember, a financial plan sets out to answer the question, where should my next dollar go? And automation can be used to put those dollars in the buckets you've decided on.

YOUR WATERFALL PLAN

Your paycheck hits. Then what? In an ideal world, you'll have automated all of your next moves. All it takes are the right data points and an hour of your time to set yourself up.

NUMBERS TO KEEP IN MIND

▷ Your take-home pay (see page 62)

▷ What accounts you have (see page 59)

▷ Your 50/20/30 breakdown (see page 68)

▷ What you need to achieve financial security (see step 3, a.k.a. the Monopoly step, page 72)

▷ What you're saving for the longer term (see step 4, page 82)

TAKE-HOME PAY (ex: $5,000)					401k (ex: $500)

Checking Account (ex: $4,000)		Emergency Fund (ex: $500)	IRA (ex: $250)	Savings Goals (ex: $250)	Other Goals (Brokerage, 529) (ex: $0)

Credit Card Payments (ex: $2,500)	Recurring Bills (utilities, gym membership, etc.) (ex: $500)

In your waterfall of funds, there are a few things I want to empha-size. First, order matters. Your dollars will go further in certain places rather than others. For example, if you get an employer match on your 401(k), that could be a 100 percent return on a dollar you save. Second, you have to find a balance. In a financial plan, you're working on a number of goals side by side.

I'm going to share how to think about automating some of the big-gest things listed on the above chart, but refer back to "Get a Plan" to home in on your unique priorities and dollar amounts to allocate.

RETIREMENT CONTRIBUTIONS

If you've decided to contribute to your 401(k) (this is a nonnegotiable!), confirm that the correct amount is being deducted from your paychecks. Not sure? Ask HR or your finance department.

If you're contributing to a retirement account outside work, you'll need to set up that contribution directly at the financial institution that holds your account.

And remember, you'll also need to automate *how* your funds are allocated. All too often, I see people who are contributing to retirement accounts but who forget (or ignore!) the next step of investing those dollars. Generally speaking, a target-date fund, a combination of stocks that takes your retirement age into account to assess risk levels, is an easy way to go.

CREDIT CARD PAYMENTS

Auto-payments are smart here, but with a caveat: you *must* check your transactions before paying. You have two choices:

1. Commit to daily money minutes, and put your credit card payments on autopilot. That way, you catch any errors before the bill is paid.
2. Set calendar reminders once a month to review your transactions, and schedule auto-payment for a day or two later.

Note: Most of us won't be able to max out all of these basic financial security goals at once. It's a juggling act. Credit card debt has insane interest rates, so I want you to prioritize debt pay-down. That said, I *do* also want you to set aside money into your emergency fund at the same time. Even if it's a nominal amount, it helps in two big ways. First, it gets you into the habit of saving (and building habits takes time!), and second, it starts to give you a cushion so that you can avoid getting into deeper levels of debt down the line.

EMERGENCY FUND CONTRIBUTIONS

Put aside a fixed amount each month, or even twice per month, toward your emergency fund goal. Remember—this goal is based on your income, so as your salary and expenses go up, you'll need to compensate for that here.

SAVINGS GOAL CONTRIBUTIONS

You've already set up sub-accounts for your savings goals. Now set up auto-contributions so that you're making progress on these goals without even thinking about it!

This might be a contribution to a 529 plan, a vacation fund, or a down payment fund. Remember to name the accounts to make saving that much more motivating.

YOUR AUTO CALENDAR ALERTS

Now that your money is automatically going into the right buckets on an ongoing basis, we're not going with a total set-it-and-forget-it approach. Rather, you need to automate calendar alerts so that you remember those key moments throughout the year when action is required. Getting the most out of your wallet is an ongoing process. You're investing critical time right now, just by reading this book, so go the extra mile and remind your future self what to do.

YOUR GUIDE TO REMINDERS

MONTHLY ALERTS	• Confirm credit card payments • Confirm bill payments
QUARTERLY ALERTS	• Money check-ins (If you're partnered, this is a check-in with your family on combined progress. If you're managing money solo, it's a reminder to pause and reevaluate your goals and progress.) • 50/20/30 budget check-ins • Check your credit score
JANUARY	• Make all tax-advantaged contributions (for example, 529, retirement accounts). By contributing at the beginning of the year, you get a full year of growth. • If a freelancer, file quarterly taxes • Find out when your employer does open enrollment, and put the date on your calendar—choosing the right benefits package at work is one of the most important things you can do! • Do your yearly assessment of your financial plan
FEBRUARY	• Prep for taxes (They're due in April, so don't procrastinate!)
MARCH	• File your taxes (Filing early means you can avoid the last-minute rush *and* get your refund faster!)
APRIL	• If a freelancer, file quarterly taxes • Annual review of your insurance policies, to make sure no life changes require additional coverage
MAY	• Get a copy of your credit report from each of the three bureaus, and check for any errors or fraud.
JUNE	• If a freelancer, file quarterly taxes
JULY	
AUGUST	
SEPTEMBER	• If a freelancer, file quarterly taxes
OCTOBER	• Budget for holidays
NOVEMEBER	
DECEMBER	

WHAT DOES NEXT-GEN AUTOMATION LOOK LIKE?

In this hack, you're nailing the basics. You're making sure your dollars automatically go into the right buckets, and you're automating reminders to take action on your money throughout the year. This is an important foundation, but I'm also excited for how future innovation will take financial automation to the next level.

I'm not the only entrepreneur who thinks we'll see big changes here. Ken Lin said, "I think that from a data perspective, from a computer perspective, and from a trust perspective, we will have some percentage of the population put their finances on autopilot in the next five years. By autopilot, I mean they will trust some platform to optimize every aspect of their finances . . . there's a lot more trust in technology. That's where we're going."

Jason Brown of Tally echoes this: "I believe my future wallet will have the ability to automatically optimize for any and all of my financial goals, whether that's paying off my loans, remodeling my home, taking my family on a nice vacation, or saving for my kids' college."

All you have to do as the consumer is to identify your financial goals and update them as they evolve. You can then leave it to technology to handle the rest. I love the founder and CEO of Betterment Jon Stein's bullish take on our future potential here. As he put it, "In ten years, your wallet will be fully digital, and everything will be automated. You won't have to worry about physically managing your accounts, figuring out how to pay bills from what accounts, etc. When my daughters graduate from college, I can't imagine that they'll ever think about how much to put in checking versus savings, or Roth versus traditional IRAs; these problems are easily solved with software. Can you imagine a future where we might have self-driving cars, but you still have to make a manual transfer to cover a bill payment? Change is coming."

YOUR ACTION ITEMS

☐ **SET UP** auto-payments for all of your core accounts, using your financial plan from chapter 3.

☐ **PUT** calendar reminders in place for ongoing moments throughout the year so you never miss a key date.

CHAPTER 7

HACK 3 //
YOUR DAILY WALLET

I've talked a lot about your wallet. But the very definition of a wallet is evolving every day. The former Facebook executive and co-founder of Fin, Sam Lessin, eloquently predicts that "wallets will be fairy tales we tell our children, like floppy disks."

In this chapter, we'll cover how to embrace the transformational shift to your digital wallet. Think of it as a primer for how to cash in by going cash-free.

PART 1. PHYSICAL MONEY

WHAT TO KEEP IN YOUR OLD-SCHOOL WALLET

While the transition to digital is happening fast, most of us still carry around a few things at all times.

YOU NEED

▷ ID (typically driver's license)

▷ $20–$100 in cash (depending on how often you use it)

▷ primary credit card (with one stashed away safely at home as backup)

▷ debit card (for easy ATM access and as a backup credit card)

▷ picture of a child or dog (a Scottish study found that 42 percent of wallets were returned on average, with that number jumping up to 88 percent if they held a baby photo and 53 percent for a dog photo)[1]

DO NOT CARRY

▷ gift cards (unless you plan to use them that day!)

▷ other IDs/sensitive info (Social Security card, passport, and so on)

CASH IN BY GOING CASH-FREE

You may be able to tell by now: I'm really not a fan of cash. Today's digital landscape is vast, and making the bulk of your transactions in cash generally does not make sense, for all sorts of reasons.

I'm not alone. In 2011, 36 percent of Americans said they used cash for most or all purchases. By 2016, that number had dropped to 24 percent. And when you zero in on millennials, that drops down even further, to 21 percent.[2] Not only are we not spending cash as frequently, but we're not even carrying it. A U.S. Bank survey found that 50 percent of people carry cash only half of the time.[3]

So what's stepping in to replace cash? For decades, credit cards have been a go-to in the American wallet. They're so commonplace that we forget they've only been around since the 1950s, when Diners Club appeared on the scene.[4]

We talked all about the pros and cons of credit cards on page 106, so you're already familiar with the perks. With rewards programs, including cash back, it's as if your whole life were on sale (even at 1 percent, I'll take it!).

Unlike cash, you can seamlessly track your credit card transactions, so you'll always have a clear understanding of your spending and a better sense of where your money is going. Plus, if you have any issues, you can dispute transactions. Not to mention, credit cards have taken away the burden of the ATM run.

On the security front, they do have one big advantage over cash: if lost, they can be replaced. Cash in a stolen wallet is bound to be gone forever, but replacing a credit card just requires a call to the bank.

At a minimum, I want you to think about optimizing your physical wallet by (1) being incredibly organized, and (2) leveraging credit cards (and their inherent incentive structure) as it makes sense for you.

PART 2. THE DIGITAL SHIFT

Credit cards are like digital money 1.0. From Apple Pay to Venmo, the technology we use to move money around is improving all the time. While digital wallets have a long way to go in terms of widespread adoption (more about that soon), nearly half of consumers now prefer digital apps over cash.[5]

WHAT *IS* A DIGITAL WALLET?

A digital wallet is essentially just your phone. With tools like Apple Pay, Google Pay, and Samsung Pay (at least one of which comes preinstalled on most phones—no download required, though you do have to manually link them to your bank account or credit card), we now have the ability to use our smartphones to move money in countless directions. Once you log in and get through your layers of password protection (ideally, PIN, fingerprint, and even facial recognition), secure access to your money is right at your fingertips.

Tyler Winklevoss, co-founder and CEO of Gemini, predicts that "in ten years our wallets will not only look and feel like our smartphones; they will *be* our smartphones." Yet if you're like the average consumer, you're likely not taking full advantage of these mobile tools to manage your money. Most of us just use the basics. According to the Federal Reserve, nearly half of U.S. consumers use their phones to access their bank accounts for simple tasks, like checking their balance.[6]

When it comes to payments, we're only just beginning to catch on. Only 24 percent of mobile phone owners report having made a mobile payment in the last year.[7] As of 2017, only 13 percent of iPhone users had even activated Apple Pay. And a study from PYMNTS.com found that less than one in twenty consumers with a digital wallet app actually uses it when the opportunity arises.[8]

So what's holding us back? People cite reasons like the ease of using cash or credit and a distrust of the new technology. But the truth is that once you get comfortable with it, mobile pay is even easier than using cash or credit, and the security risks are negligible, as long as your phone itself is protected. Here's how Apple explains it:[9]

▷ It's faster than a credit or debit card, saving you time at checkout.

▷ It's more secure, because your card number is never even given to the merchant.

▷ It's more anonymous, because they don't store transaction info that's tied to you.

Going a layer deeper, Apple Pay uses something called NFC technology, which stands for "near-field communication." NFC is a way of wirelessly transmitting data via a chip built into your phone. The chip transmits data without you ever having to reach for your card.[10]

This is the same technology that some banks are now using to enable cardless ATMs. It seems hard to believe, but you can now withdraw cash without your trusty debit card: you just tap your phone, enter your PIN, and that's it. Chase, for example, started rolling out the feature in 2016 and by 2018 announced that it was live at nearly all sixteen thousand Chase ATMs.[11]

To understand what a time-saver this can be, imagine you run out to do some errands. When you get to the store, you realize you left your wallet at home. All you have is your phone.

Before digital wallets, you would have had no choice but to return home and get your wallet—an annoyance and big waste of time. But today, you have two options: First, see if the store accepts Apple/Google/Samsung Pay. (Tons of major retailers do, from Trader Joe's to Best Buy to Staples.) Or, if an in-store digital payment isn't an option, you can head to your nearest ATM and simply swipe your phone to access your debit account. Seconds later, you'll have cash in hand to make your purchase.

This is tremendously powerful. Technology has made it so that the only physical thing you need to buy something is your phone—which you're already likely to have on hand, considering that nearly eight in ten Americans have a smartphone, and we rarely leave home without them.[12]

I believe it's only a matter of time before digital wallets take over and that eventually everything from our driver's licenses to our health insurance cards will exist in digital form. If this sounds far-fetched, consider that it used to be wild to think that a plastic credit card could represent and be used in place of real, physical dollars. And yet today most of us can't imagine a world without credit cards.

Plus, we're going mobile in all other aspects of our lives: movie theaters, concert venues, and sporting arenas all support mobile ticketing, and a third of airline boarding passes are soon to be mobile.[13] In other words, gone are the days in which losing our boarding pass on our way to the gate or dropping our ticket stub while waiting on line at the concession stand meant potentially missing our flight (or show or ball game); now we just whip out our phone, scan, and go. The value proposition of "fast, simple, and secure" is just too irresistible not to catch on.

WHAT DOES THIS MEAN FOR CREDIT CARDS?

I think it's super interesting to consider what this might mean for the credit card industry. Currently, platforms like Apple Pay require you to link a credit (or debit) card, and for now you're incentivized to do that—while using Apple Pay, you're still racking up credit card points. But businesses pay a price in the form of credit card transaction fees. The average U.S. business (with revenue between $10,000 and $250,000) pays 2.87–4.35 percent on each and every credit card transaction.[14]

So, what if businesses cut out credit card processors and passed those savings on to the consumer? Instead of drawing from your credit, your "digital wallet" would simply transfer money seamlessly from your account over to a vendor. It's not impossible to imagine cutting credit cards out of the equation—putting the onus on the business to incentivize consumers, likely in the form of perks and savings.

PEER-TO-PEER (P2P) PAYMENTS: VENMO, ZELLE, AND BEYOND

Another digital payment method that is picking up steam is something called peer-to-peer, or P2P, payments. Instead of streamlining the way we transfer money to a business like Google and Apple Pay do, P2P apps provide a seamless way for us to pass money on to another individual or other individuals, no cash required.

When you think about these types of digital payments, your mind is likely to go straight to the industry leader, Venmo. Known to be one of the most popular money apps among millennials, Venmo now has a commonly recognized catchphrase: "I'll Venmo you!" It's popularity is due in part, perhaps, to the social element it has built in. PayPal, which owns Venmo, revealed that more than 90 percent of transactions are open to friends or the public, and the same amount includes some message or emoji.[15]

Other players in the space include Cash, which is owned by Square and boasted seven million active users in December 2017, and Zelle, a platform offered by a number of U.S. banks that has seen nearly 100,000 people sign up every day.[16]

While these apps are still evolving, they have made it exponentially easier for people to pass money back and forth. Splitting the bill at dinner, for example, has long been the subject of etiquette debate. And while P2P payments don't resolve the age-old question of *how* to split the bill (divide it evenly versus everyone pays for what he or she ordered), it does make the execution a whole lot easier. Now diners don't have to worry about having the exact amount of change, or nag the one friend who never seems to have cash to pay them back. Everyone can literally sit around a table, while one person pays and everyone else sends her the correct amount of money, in real time and down to the penny.

The amount of money flowing through P2P payments is vast: In the first quarter of 2018, Venmo processed over $12 billion in transactions, and Zelle processed $25 billion[17]—but how do they work?

It's fairly simple. You link your bank or credit card account to the app. To pay a friend, simply look him up on your app of choice (using a cell phone number is an easy way to find a person), enter an amount, and hit "send" (you can also do the same to request funds, but this just triggers a nudge, rather than an actual transaction). Money typically hits your friend's P2P app account instantly, but apps vary in terms of how quickly users can transfer in-app balances to their bank. For example, it can take Venmo a business day or two for a balance to be transferred to a checking account, but Zelle, because the app works directly with banks, transfers money into your checking account instantly.

WHAT TO KNOW ABOUT P2P: SECURITY AND FEES

Going back to Apple Pay's promise to be fast, simple, and secure, P2P apps get high marks in the first two categories. There are two big things to look out for here: security and fees.

On the security front, financial experts (myself included) recommend using P2P networks with trusted people only. *And* double-checking that you're paying the correct person. Unlike with credit cards, once that money has been sent, it's out there.

In terms of fees, remember to read the fine print—and to continue doing so! Fee structures for these types of platforms, particularly new ones, will change as companies figure out how to monetize. Venmo, for example, has been known to charge fees for instant transfers (currently twenty-five cents) and for the use of credit cards instead of a checking account (currently a 3 percent charge).

One other thing to consider is what P2P apps mean for peer-to-peer relationships. Michael Norton points to research from his colleagues Tami Kim and Ting Zhang which shows that "one downside [of P2P apps] is that these new forms of connecting consumers can erode social capital and connection . . . the simple act of using payment apps like Venmo can cause friends to start seeing each other as petty ('You're really going to make me pay you exactly $21.34?'), whereas without such apps friends round up or down ('You can just pay me $20')—a sign that the friendship is communal, not transactional."

As these technologies evolve, we can't forget that money is often personal. There are tremendous pros to using P2P—like ease of use and the app's inherent record keeping—but there's a psychological shift happening too.

THE PSYCHOLOGY OF DIGITAL MONEY

As we shift away from cash payments, we do need to pause and consider how digital methods impact the psychology of our spending more broadly.

Many studies have shown that we have a harder time parting with cold hard cash than a credit card swipe, and the bigger the bill, the bigger the pain of handing it to the cashier. In 2014, for example, research out of Iowa State University found, through a variety of experiments, that we spend less when using cash as compared with credit cards.[18] But *why*? Is it because a credit card feels more abstract? Or that we only have to reach for one card as opposed to a stack of bills? The fact that there's a delay in the funds leaving our possession permanently?

The study reached an interesting conclusion: "It was the action of counting out the cash payment, and not the appearance of the cash itself, that reduced spending." To get here, they asked participants to go through an online payment portal using three different payment methods: images of cash that participants had to drag and drop, images of cash "tokens" marked with payment denominations that participants had to drag and drop, and credit cards. There was no significant difference in spending between the images of cash versus the cash "tokens," but subjects spent far less with these two forms of payment than with credit cards. Crazy, right? It's not the fact that we perceive cash to be inherently more valuable than a credit card; it's the act of counting it that makes it harder to part with.

So how does this impact us as consumers? First of all, the study argues, digital interfaces matter. A lot. By taking the counting out of the equation, modern e-commerce platforms may be encouraging us to spend more.

Look no further than the example of Square's tipping screen to recognize how your spending might also be impacted by this phenomenon. Square defaults to three options, 15 percent, 20 percent, 25 percent, plus "no tip." When you're standing across from a cashier, the pressure to tip is unavoidable (a phenomenon so widespread it's even been labeled guilt tipping).

While you might not have counted out that 20 percent in cash and dropped it in the jar at the coffee shop, it only takes a quick tap to add 20 percent to your total. Between 2012 and 2013, Square saw shoppers add tips to 37 percent more transactions. We're not just tipping more; we're tipping in cases we never used to.[19]

Don't get me wrong: tipping is something I value. My point is not to become stingy here. That said, as digital platforms like Square become ubiquitous (who would have thought you could so seamlessly use credit at a farmers' market?), it's worth recognizing that every payment system we use is deliberately designed to encourage spending. Companies employ entire teams of UX and UI—tech acronyms for "user experience" and "user interface"—designers for that very purpose. The more we can understand about how interfaces affect our brains, the savvier consumers we become.

THE "PAIN OF PAYING"

How do we embrace technology while maintaining financial security? Some of the most interesting thoughts on the topic come from the behavioral economist Dan Ariely.[20] He explains that we're all subject to the "pain of paying."

Here's his classic example: You go to a nice dinner at a restaurant where you know the prices. When the bill comes, you're not surprised by the total. Would you rather pay in cash or credit? According to Ariely, cash feels worse, and for some the "pain of paying" can suck the joy right out of the whole experience. A credit card only somewhat removes the agony of seeing those dollars disappear before our eyes.

At the crux of Ariely's work is this: "The timing and method of payment affects enjoyment." Ariely went so far as to test this on his Duke PhD students, quickly verifying that if there's one way to ruin pizza, it's by making diners hand over cash with each bite.

That simple concept gives us the power to fundamentally alter how we feel about spending. Ariely wisely points out that there are times when you'll want to decrease the pain of paying, but there are also times to increase it. If you're struggling with credit card debt, for example, a little pain might help you stick to your budget.

At the same time, I'm a big believer in spending money on experiences. And if you work hard all week to save up for a nice dinner on Friday night, don't you deserve to actually enjoy it? One of the most effective methods of decreasing the pain, Ariely says, is prepayment. If you've ever gone on one of those all-inclusive vacations, you know that $20 cocktail tastes much better when it's already covered than it does when you're handed the check the second you're done.

You can adopt this psychology proactively in your own life. Because you have a financial plan, you've automated much of the thought and strategy behind your spending. You already know what you can afford, so if you've budgeted $500 or $1,000 or $5,000 to take a vacation, there's zero harm in prepaying for all your flights, hotels, and maybe even meals in advance. Yes, parting with your cash before a trip is a bit risky, but it's not financially irresponsible.

So, prepay for your next trip. Buy packages of workout class credits, and remove the pain of paying when you go to class. Venmo friends for group dinners before they even happen. Today, more than ever, when and how you pay is often within your control.

YOUR ACTION ITEMS

☐ **AUDIT** your physical wallet, and make sure you're only carrying the essentials. Add in a dog or baby pic to increase the likelihood of it being returned if lost!

☐ **DOWNLOAD** apps for your financial institutions so you can take advantage of basics like checking your account balances.

☐ **SET UP YOUR DIGITAL WALLET ON YOUR PHONE.** Scan your debit and credit cards into your phone's pay app, and see if your bank offers cardless ATMs.

☐ **LOOK INTO PEER-TO-PEER APPS.** If you don't have one, ask friends (those you'd be transacting with most) which app they use before making your selection. If you are already using these apps, make sure your account is set up properly to minimize fees (for example, connected to a checking account, not a credit card).

☐ **KEEP AN EYE ON SPENDING.** Digital wallets have a tremendous upside, but if overspending is a challenge for you, pay attention to psychological factors—like the method and timing of payment or the type of digital interface—that might be at play.

CHAPTER 8

HACK 4 //
SMART SHOPPING

In the spirit of saving time and money, smart shopping is high on the list of wins. I mean "smart" in all senses of the word. It refers to the growing class of devices that use powerful machine-learning technology to tailor experiences to its user and the environment (see smart car, smartphone, and so on), and it's savvy.

Remember, time is money. Given the tools at our fingertips, it doesn't make a ton of sense to run errands. After all, there's technology that can know when we're out of paper towels or breakfast cereal or toothpaste before we do—not to mention our preferred brand and whether it's on sale. It's time to utilize it to help us put time back into our day and cash back into our wallets.

To show you what I mean by "smart shopping," let's get personal. There are some key ways I've optimized my Amazon Prime account, and it's easy for you to do the same. I'm not here to shill for the company, but the truth is that Amazon's customer-centric business model makes it the "smart" place to go to get the best deals around. As a parent, I'm particularly grateful to be living during this era of shopping innovation, because nothing puts more of a crunch on your time and money than having kids!

KEEP BASICS BASIC

Like it or not, we all have value systems around money (many of which were formed during our childhoods). Personally, I love spending on experiences and travel, and I prioritize being generous with family and friends. But I hate to spend more than I absolutely have to on the boring basics.

So I bifurcate the way I think about my shopping: Basics go into one category. I want them to be as cheap as possible! In the other category are the things I actually enjoy and care about, and I invest more time and money there. Based on the countless conversations I've had with people about their finances over the years, I know I'm not alone in these priorities. This chapter is about how to optimize our shopping around the things we care about.

PUT HOUSEHOLD SHOPPING ON AUTOPILOT

As it stands, you probably already buy the same exact type of dish detergent, orange juice, and sandwich bags every time you head to the store. So the first step in automating your shopping is to take the time up front to set up subscriptions for the basic things your family needs.

Why subscriptions? The answer is savings. It's no wonder that as of 2017 nineteen million people had leveraged Amazon's Subscribe & Save program:[1] Amazon offers a perk through Amazon Prime whereby if you subscribe and purchase at least five items on an automatically recurring basis, you get 15 percent off. For certain items, like diapers and baby food, that jumps up to 20 percent off, thanks to a program called Amazon Family. And Amazon isn't alone in this: companies like Target, Chewy, and Walgreens offer discounts up to 20 percent for signing up for recurring shipments. Plus, with a subscription, cleaning supplies, paper towels, diapers, toothpaste, shampoo, conditioner, and so on show up right at my door each month, and I don't ever have to think about it (or run out of them!). I then check in at least once a month to ensure that everything we're getting next month is still something we need and to ensure the quantities are accurate. Setting this all up took only an hour, and I never have to think about it. Essentially, my basics are now all 15–20 percent off, shipped to me for free, and I get hours of time back per month! I consider that a triple win.

Next, I did the same thing with AmazonFresh. If you spend at least $50 per week (which isn't hard for a family of four), you trigger free shipping. It's the same approach here: I went through and picked out all of the items that are high quality, healthy, and well priced for my family. Over time, I've picked a favorite out of all the items I could ever need, so I can easily create new shopping carts from my past purchases. Each week, I go in and literally "grocery shop" a week's worth of food for my whole family in under five minutes. I check off some boxes, hit "enter", and move on!

I've now saved the hassle of making those choices (decision fatigue is real), and I didn't have to trek to a store where I was beholden to its prices. Unfortunately, you rarely get the best price by walking into a store. For example, canned tomatoes at the store a block from my home are $3.99. On Amazon, they're $1.99. A gallon of organic milk is $6.99 at the local store, and $3.99 on Amazon—plus, no schlepping required.

There are a ton of tools in this category of smart shopping, and they don't start and end with groceries. You can order just about anything you would find at your local Walmart from Jetblack, car care products on CarPro, and much more. Go to page 184 for the full list.

SIDE NOTE: It's worth mentioning that there are environmental costs of the gas it takes to deliver something to your doorstep (though it's just in lieu of your being on the road yourself), plus an overuse of packaging. Do consider this as you think about the frequency of your shopping and the retailers you choose. Ideally, you do things in bulk!

SHOP SEASONALLY

If it sounds like I'm uninterested in shopping altogether, I'm not. I just prefer to invest my time shopping for things I actually enjoy. That's where shopping seasonally comes in. It takes a bit of planning and foresight, but if you can time your purchases wisely, you'll save big.

What do I mean by that? All too often, we make purchases right when we need something—laptops for back-to-school season, winter coats when it snows, AC units in the summer. But that is precisely the time when retailers can charge full prices for items, because demand is simply higher.

For years, I've followed this simple calendar to help time any of my major shopping decisions. For fans of *Financially Fearless*, this may ring a bell, but the advice still holds true. Here's what to buy when, and—pro tip!—consider putting reminders on your calendar to shop seasonally for things you know you'll need in the next year. Consider this a smart addition to the reminder calendar you already ran through on page 119.

WHAT TO BUY WHEN

JANUARY	FEBRUARY	MARCH
Winter boots, clothing, and coats; suits; perfume; home furnishings; carpets and flooring; big appliances; linens and bedding; holiday supplies; office furniture	Winter boots, clothing, and coats; perfume; home renovations; bicycles; cameras; home entertainment systems	Sweaters and cashmere; china and flatware; air conditioners; gas grills; gardening tools

APRIL	MAY	JUNE
Sweaters and cashmere; sneakers; vacuum cleaners; snowblowers; office furniture; cruises; electronics	Vacuum cleaners; cookware; refrigerators; big appliances; grilling supplies; small kitchen appliances; electronics; mattresses and box springs	Men's suits; tools; cookware; paint; champagne and sparkling wine; gym memberships

JULY	AUGUST	SEPTEMBER
Suits; furniture; big appliances	School supplies; trees, shrubs, and plants; lawn mowers; computers	China and flatware; wine; computers; jeans; cars; holiday airfare

OCTOBER	NOVEMBER	DECEMBER
Swimsuits; big appliances; dining room furniture; mattresses and box springs; air conditioners; gas grills; school supplies; cars	Wedding dresses; cookware; Christmas trees; toys; electronics	Televisions; pools; small kitchen appliances

Source: Adapted from *Financially Fearless*

YOUR ACTION ITEMS

☐ **LIST** the basics you need for your home, and go on a research mission to find the best products and price compare.

☐ **AUTOMATE** the delivery of these items to your home, making sure to maximize that 15–20 percent savings from subscriptions.

☐ **SET** calendar reminders for any big purchases you foresee making over the next year, based on the seasonal calendar.

CHAPTER 9

HACK 5 //
PROTECTING YOUR HARD-EARNED CASH

Delta. Macy's. Target. Yahoo. Equifax.

What do these companies have in common? They've all made headlines for exposing customer data, thanks to security breaches.

Just as you're working hard to earn those dollars, hackers around the globe are trying to access them. According to a 2016 study by the Pew Research Center, the majority of Americans (six in ten!) have been the victim of a major data breach. That includes everything from fraudulent credit card charges (good motivation for those daily money minutes), to hacked social media accounts, to falsified lines of credit.[1]

With proper protections in place, these security issues should not deter you from going digital. But they do mean that you need to be vigilant and set yourself up to keep your personal information as secure as possible. I've had tons of people in my life who have had some issue with financial fraud or identity theft. If you're properly monitoring your money, you'll know within hours (or even minutes) if something is amiss, and you can take steps to minimize the damage. Finding issues quickly will save you a massive headache down the line.

Sheldon Cuffie, Chief Information Security Officer at Northwestern Mutual, explains, "Internet safety is very similar to personal and physical safety. Know your surroundings and take reasonable precautions to protect yourself digitally. While you can't see a potential digital attacker, you can make yourself a more difficult target utilizing simple actions. This fits into a broader narrative of personal resilience, of which digital resilience is now a significant part of the equation."

Sure, with new technologies in place, there are new entry points for digital attacks. But technology also gives us new ways of protecting ourselves, too. Ken Lin, CEO of Credit Karma, explains, "We have come a long way as an industry and society over the last twenty years with regard to identity theft. It's become more common, and as a result the remediation on those issues is more straightforward. We should be diligent and aware, but we should not be so fearful." So with that in mind, while security matters, it should not hold you back from taking advantage of the amazing tools out there.

•

HOW TO PROTECT YOURSELF EVERY DAY

PASSWORD PROTECT

When it comes to discussing financial security, passwords are key (pun intended). Just like locking your door, the goal is to prevent people from accessing your most valuable personal possession: your info. So how do you create a strong password?

USE A PASSWORD MANAGER

A lot is at stake here, but why shoulder the burden yourself if you don't have to? Password managers are a simple way to store multiple passwords across a variety of platforms. Companies like Dashlane,

Keeper, LastPass, and Blur offer free options or subscription-based models that get high marks for security.[2]

Cuffie recommends utilizing one of these tools, both for their security features and for sheer convenience. "In many cases, you don't even need to know what the password is if you copy it from your secure app directly into the website."

Password managers are particularly helpful if you're following the best practice of using different passwords for every site. I know, that sounds like a hassle. But I strongly recommend it. To see why, consider this common hacking scenario: When data is stolen from a company, like in the Target breach, hackers will often sit on that data for years. Then they'll use the info they have on you and try it on other sites. Was your Target password the same as your bank password? Boom: that hacker could now have direct access to your money. But not if you're diversifying your passwords.

MORE IS MORE

When you create passwords, complexity is critical. Having an easy-to-remember password may save you short-term headache, but it can lead to some long-term pain if you get hacked.

Strong passwords are random ones, and you should avoid including obvious personal info, like an address or birthdate.[3] In addition, Cuffie recommends passwords that are *at least* twelve characters—a combination of words, numbers, and special characters. For example, he says, "Something like 'chocolate!cowinameadow29' is easy for me to remember, and it will take seventy-six sextillion years to crack." He means that literally. Check out howsecureismypassword.net to find out how long it would take a computer to figure out your password.

TWO-FACTOR AUTHENTICATION

When given the option to protect via two-factor or multifactor authentication, always opt in. Multifactor authentication tools ask users to verify their identity via two means of verification; think of it as kind of like having to show two forms of ID. So, for example, if I enter a password onto a site, the system will prompt me to verify my identity via a text message, too.

While it might seem redundant, taking the extra moment to provide a second verification can help protect you against rogue actions. A hacker might have guessed your birthday, but if he doesn't have your cell phone number, that could save you a world of trouble.

SECURE YOUR NETWORK

Your router is your gateway out to the world, but it's also a gateway into your wallet, if it falls into a hacker's hands. Be sure to secure your own Wi-Fi network and router with a strong password to prevent network hacks that could expose your personal data (not to mention prevent your pesky neighbor from accessing your Netflix account and chilling on your bandwidth).[4]

BEWARE WHEN USING PUBLIC WI-FI

Be wary of accessing your financial data when using public Wi-Fi networks. You might want to skip taking a money minute at your local coffee shop, for example. The accessibility of public Wi-Fi is great, but you're not the only one with access to it. Hackers will use public Wi-Fi networks to exploit sensitive information and gain access to your bank accounts.

Cuffie recommends using a personal virtual private network to add a layer of security when you need to access your money away from home or work.

In addition, the Federal Communications Commission has a few key tips: make sure every website has "https" (with the *s* standing for "secure") at the beginning of the address if you're submitting personal info, change your phone settings so that you don't automatically connect to Wi-Fi, and use your data plan over Wi-Fi when sharing sensitive info.[5]

DON'T OVERSHARE

Through social media, we've gotten quite comfortable sharing intimate details of our lives with the world at large. Cuffie advises that you make sure you're utilizing the privacy controls within social media platforms—particularly around limiting permissions for unknown third-party apps. In addition, limit the amount of personally identifiable information you provide on a profile—like your home address or middle name.

USE SECURITY APPS

There are a whole host of apps out there designed to help protect you and your devices. Cuffie highlights two of his favorite categories: Because some advertisements include malware, he recommends downloading ad blocker apps on mobile devices. If you have children, Cuffie recommends leveraging "parental control" apps, like Net Nanny and FamilyTime. These apps are designed to let children freely use a phone while still keeping information safe; they come with extra security features.

HOW DO BREACHES HAPPEN?

To give you a taste of what these privacy breaches look like, let's do a deep dive into what happened with Equifax—one of the largest breaches to date.[6]

THE STORY

In 2017, Equifax (one of the three major credit bureaus, alongside Experian and TransUnion) announced that its systems had been hacked. From May through July 2017, hackers gained access to personal data from *143 million* people—including their names, Social Security numbers, and addresses.[7] As if that weren't bad enough, Equifax revealed in 2018 that at least another 2 million consumers had been affected.[8]

The breach all came down to a tech vulnerability—specifically, an error in an open-source framework it used for its web app called Apache Struts 2. A "patch" to fix the vulnerability had been released in March 2017, but Equifax didn't make the required update, leaving its software open to attack.[9]

How did the hackers feign access to the code in the first place? Well, the "open" in "open source" refers to the fact that anyone can access them; it's a way for an unlimited number of developers from anywhere in the world to contribute code and collaborate on projects. But that means it also allows bad actors to collaborate on exposing security vulnerabilities. Generally speaking, these hacks are preventable via patches released to improve the software's security. However, if the company housing your data falls behind in updates as Equifax did, it puts consumers at risk.

WHAT YOU CAN DO

The Equifax data breach affected roughly half of the U.S. population. Needless to say, the widespread impact led both Equifax and Congress to take aggressive steps to help consumers minimize the damage. In the wake of the breach, the company established a website to allow you to confirm if your personal data was exposed, and offered a free annual subscription to credit monitoring to protect and alert you against suspicious activity.[10]

HOW TO PROTECT YOURSELF AFTER A BREACH

If you suspect you've been hacked, the first step is to alert your bank(s) and credit card companies and make sure they are on the lookout for suspicious activity and issue you all new credit and debit cards. Additionally, you should do the following:

BE WARY OF UNKNOWN PHONE CALLS

Have you missed a call from a strange, unknown number? Sure, it could be your long-lost cousin, but it's certainly not the compromised company calling you to resolve the issue. When widespread breaches happen, scammers will often call and try to get you to verify personal information by phone—another hack in and of itself. The Federal Trade Commission issued a warning after Equifax and recommends that you never provide personal info unless you initiate the phone call. Caller ID can be spoofed too, so be wary of whether callers are who they claim to be.[11]

MONITOR YOUR ACCOUNTS

You know how to take a money minute. When your accounts are linked to a personal financial management app, your regular reviews can help you quickly identify whether something is up. It's one thing to read the news of a breach and check your accounts immediately, but I want you to take the extra step and continue to keep a close eye on the reality of your finances for the long term.

SET UP FRAUD ALERTS

If you're looking to verify that no new, unknown activity is occurring with your money, a fraud alert is a good place to start. Fraud alerts require companies to verify your identity before issuing credit, making it hard for a scammer to take out credit in your name.

You can tailor fraud alerting to fit your security needs and your lifestyle. Initial fraud alerting will last for at least ninety days and allow you to renew alerts after that, while extended fraud alerting will last for seven years. If you're an active-duty service member, there are even ways to enable fraud alerting for one year while you or a loved one is deployed.[12]

To set one up, simply contact one of the three credit reporting bureaus (Experian, TransUnion, or Equifax), and ask whichever one you call to alert the others.

These tips are simple but impactful. To go even deeper, you can find tons of info for ongoing best practices around security at sites like ConnectSafely.org. The above should be sufficient to keep you safe, but if you have reasons to worry further (like a past breach that impacted you), consider monitoring services like LifeLock.

Remember, I want you to make the most out of digital benefits and ultimately trust technology to help you better your finances.

YOUR ACTION ITEMS

☐ **UPDATE** your passwords to be more secure, and set up a password manager to make remembering them extra easy.

☐ **SET UP** multifactor authentication on your accounts, especially for your email account, bank accounts, and social media accounts.

☐ **DOWNLOAD** apps to keep your mobile device safe, including an ad blocker and a parental control app (if you have kids).

CHAPTER 10

HACK 6 //
RAISING DIGITAL WALLET NATIVES

As I write this book, I have two children under the age of four. While I haven't been parenting for long, I have been thinking about parenting and money for over a decade. We know how deeply rooted our money values and habits are and how often they continue to crop up throughout our lives. They impact the purchasing decisions we make, how well we save, how we manage our finances as a couple, and once we become parents, they impact the values and habits we instill in our kids, whether consciously or not.

A 2018 study from the University of Michigan found that children have formed spending behaviors when they're *as young as five*.[1] So clearly, teaching your children about money isn't something that can wait until they get their first job. You have to start early.

As modern parents, we have a unique challenge: our children are poised to be digital wallet natives. Using their phone to make a purchase, a PFM to monitor their account balances, and a P2P app to exchange money with just about anyone will be the norm and largely how they learn to transact. Remember how Sam Lessin predicted wallets will be akin to floppy disks? Think of cash as a cassette tape and credit cards as CDs.

Simple things, like giving your child an allowance in cash, will likely become a thing of the past. We don't know exactly what the future will look like, but there's no doubt it will be different for our kids than it was for us. And while the evolution of money over the past fifty years was slow enough to give us ample time to adapt, technology is forcing us to move faster than ever before.

In light of this changing landscape, what we *can* zero in on is how to instill core money values and habits in our kids that set them up for success—no matter what money looks and feels like for them. Here are a few ways I—and other parents I know and respect—try to do just that.

THE MARSHMALLOW TEST

I studied psychology in college, and so I'm guessing that anyone who's taken Psych 101 will be familiar with the famous "Marshmallow Test." First done at Stanford in the 1960s, the study tested the long-term effects of delayed gratification in children. The setup was simple. Kids were told that they could have one marshmallow now or two later. The researchers then tracked these children into adulthood and found that the ones who delayed gratification and waited for the marshmallow grew up to be more successful and competent overall.

There were many factors that played into the results, but perhaps we could learn a thing or two from those kids who waited for the second marshmallow. Why? Because delayed gratification is one of the most powerful tools in your financial planning arsenal. It's all about thinking about and saving for future goals that we can enjoy at some point down the road.

That's why I, as a parent, care so much about teaching my kids this valuable skill. My daughter Toby actually has *five* physical piggy banks in her bedroom. They range from massive to tiny, and the size of the bank correlates to the size of the goal she is saving for. The biggest one is for college savings, moving down to a bike, then to charity, and all the way down to treats (like a cupcake or ice cream). Every few days or so, we put money in one of them—perhaps because she's done something great or found a quarter. When the big piggy banks fill up, we take a trip to the local bank and deposit the money into a savings account.

Multiple piggy banks means that each time she has a quarter to "deposit," she gets to choose which goal to put it toward, which teaches her to be more thoughtful and intentional about saving, and it's good preparation for real life, where we are constantly making choices and trade-offs about what to save for. Ron Joelson, Chief Investment Officer at Northwestern Mutual, advocates for this multi-piggy-bank strategy and advises, "Make sure they don't feel guilty about spending what they have saved for spending if they want to. Ask them each week if the 'allocation' seems right. Talk to them about why they are making the choices they are making; that's an early lesson in rebalancing!"

At three, Toby is still too young to understand "college savings," but she sure knows ice cream. Plus, she enjoys the process, which is part of the point. As she grows and earns her own money, I want her to have positive memories associated with saving and feel empowered to make her own decisions about spending.

I also *love* the strategy Randi Zuckerberg, CEO of Zuckerberg Media and author of the children's book *Dot*, uses with her seven-year-old. He gets a weekly allowance for as many dollars as his age (that is, $7 at age seven). He's allowed to spend it anytime, but at the end of the month Zuckerberg doubles whatever he hasn't spent. "I want to teach him that if you save your money, it works for you," she explains.

"I want to show him that if he holds on to his money, and it doesn't burn a hole in his pocket to spend right away, great things can happen. He saw that after a year of saving, he was able to buy himself a $300 Nintendo switch. A seven-year-old bought that because he learned how to save up."

MAKE HONESTY YOUR POLICY

My husband and I made a critical pact with each other long before there was even an actual child in the picture: that we would talk about money in front of our (future) kids and do it in a matter-of-fact way, the way we would talk about chores or a visit to the playground. We want them to understand that money is simply a tool; it's not meant to be worshipped or ignored.

How do you do that in practice? Let's say you're saving for a family vacation. Share that. Explain why you're doing it, and how. Let them in on the experience. You don't have to get into real numbers, but talk through the decisions you're making.

And when times are tough financially, talk to them about it—in an age-appropriate way of course. It's tempting to want to shield our kids from the fact that we're struggling, but trust me, your kids will pick up on the tension anyway. It's much better to be open about this part of life than to leave them scared and confused about what's going on.

SHOW THE VALUE OF HARD WORK

With our piggy bank strategy and open conversations, we're trying to introduce Toby to real adult life as early as possible (one could say we're trying to adapt "adulting" for the three-year-old set). And there's no adult lesson more valuable than the importance of hard work.

Of course, we're not the first parents to try to teach our kids the association between hard work and earning income; many of us grew up getting an allowance *after* finishing our chores. I am a firm believer in this practice; after all, what is our job as parents if not to prepare our children for real life? Simply handing a kid $10 for no reason doesn't mimic real life at all. The designer and entrepreneur Rebecca Minkoff says, "I like to make my kids 'earn their toys.' I often give them extra jobs around the house, and it teaches them that they have to work for things they want. Remember that a small job to you might seem like a big job to them, so take it at a gradient."

I also believe in showing kids that hard work has intangible value, too—that it's not *just* about saving up for that cupcake or that bike. When I leave for work in the morning, and Toby doesn't want me to go, we talk about why I'm leaving. Even though she's only a toddler, she knows that "hard work" is important to me and valued within our family.

Associating money with work is one part of the equation. The other is instilling responsibility in how they spend that money. Daphne Oz recommends, "Whether you want to give them a weekly allowance, or pay them for chores, give them a chance to have something that is theirs, and then present them with opportunities to make choices with their money, where they can see what happens with a finite resource and also start to feel their own sense of security and control."

LEAD BY EXAMPLE

Here's one thing I've learned as a parent: kids are surprisingly perceptive. They see everything you do, and they absorb everything they see, at least on some level. So when we talk about parenting and money, it's important to focus not only on what values to instill in your children but also on your own actions here.

Jon Stein, CEO of Betterment, says, "Whenever my wife and I take our two daughters shopping or out to eat with us, we like to have them pay with cash to teach them the value of the dollar. It's a great lesson for them to see that in order to get something, you have to give up something. If we pay with a card, we talk about how we earned the money that we're now spending. Nothing comes free or 'with the swipe of a card.' Purchases are earned."

Modeling good money habits matters throughout your kids' lives.

When you have teens, it's vital that you open a credit card for them to allow them to start building credit. Let them fully into the process so you can have simple but frank discussions about how *you* use credit, why it matters, and how they should think about it (like a loan you pay off in full each month, not free rein to spend). Melanie Whelan recalls she thought her dad was crazy when he told her, at age seventeen, to start saving for retirement, but now she realizes that "as usual he was right! Financial advice can be complicated, but as with most things sometimes the simplest advice is the best," she says.

Another example you can set is to open a 529 plan to save for college, and let them see you flex your savings muscle to help it grow. Skip a few small gifts over the years, and instead make regular deposits toward college savings. You can ask the same of any family or friends; they'll be happy to make a contribution to your kid's savings as a birthday present in lieu of a new toy. These small gifts over a decade can turn into real, significant savings.

Luckily, there are a lot of tools to take willpower out of this equation. On the 529 front, in addition to automatic savings contributions, there are a number of apps that can help. Grandparents and family, for example, can contribute to a 529 via Ugift, and there are a number of other apps listed on page 187.

Of course, this isn't a book about parenting, and I don't assume that what works for my family will necessarily work for yours. At its core, my advice is simple: talk to your kids about money and teach them good habits from a young age. They're listening, watching, and learning, even in their earliest years.

YOUR ACTION ITEMS

☐ **ESTABLISH** an age-appropriate allowance system and family-oriented ways to learn about saving.

☐ **MAKE** money an active conversation. When times are good or bad, include your children so they develop an adult relationship with money themselves.

☐ **SET UP** a tool like Ugift to empower your whole family to save toward meaningful goals.

THE FUTURE OF MONEY

What will the future of money look like? I wish I had a crystal ball to help answer that. Unfortunately, I don't own one of those, but here's one thing I do know: we are entering entirely uncharted territory when it comes to technology, and especially when it comes to technology and your money. And even when we have a sense of the advances and breakthroughs that lie ahead, trying to predict how they'll be used is another story altogether. As Michael J. Casey, senior adviser at the MIT Media Lab, put it in the documentary *Explained*, we couldn't have foreseen that Uber would be an outcome of the internet, just as I can't foresee all the future uses for the many financial innovations emerging today.

One of the reasons I believe so much in innovation is that on the whole it tends to empower everyday consumers. As we've seen throughout this book, innovation can put more money, more time, and more efficiency back into your life.

So let's break down some of the innovations that are swirling around so far: crypto, blockchain, Bitcoin; I'm sure you've heard of them all. I'll explain what these are all about and share where experts think the trends are heading and how these innovations may transform our lives.

Whatever happens, the next chapter of our digital money is just now being written. Kind of exciting, isn't it?

Warning: While I think it's critical to understand crypto and blockchain as a category that will impact our lives, running out to buy Bitcoin is not what I'd call your first financial priority—far from it. But these new forms of currency are out there, and I want to make sure you are well informed.

CHAPTER 11

DECODING BLOCKCHAIN

As an entrepreneur who has spent a lot of time working in FinTech, I can tell you that the concept of cryptocurrency is still deeply mystifying to most people, including us in finance.

Of course, that doesn't stop people from buzzing about crypto and its many incarnations—Bitcoin, Ethereum, and so on—everywhere from backyard barbecues to boardrooms. While it definitely involves a ton of buzzwords, the chatter isn't all just overblown hype. I—along with many other experts—believe that this foundational technology could profoundly change how we think about money.

In this chapter, I'll share the basics of blockchain and the cryptocurrency universe, breaking down the jargon, the history, and the truth-is-stranger-than-fiction story of crypto's meteoric rise. This chapter's foundation is key to understanding all the ways this breakthrough technology may change our wallets in the future, which we'll get to in the Conclusion.

Let's dive in.

YOUR CRYPTO DICTIONARY

The technology that underlies cryptocurrency is complex, and it comes with tons of confusing jargon. Before we go any further, I want to give you a go-to reference for the vocab that I'll use in the following pages. I've decoded everything in plain English, and where applicable I've included the official dictionary definitions—courtesy of *Merriam-Webster*, which added much of this crypto vocab in March 2018.[1] Refer back to this anytime an unknown word pops up!

NEW LINGO	FORMAL DEFINITION	HOW I UNDERSTAND IT
Cryptocurrency	"Any form of currency that only exists digitally, that usually has no central issuing or regulating authority but instead uses a decentralized system to record transactions and manage the issuance of new units, and that relies on cryptography to prevent counterfeiting and fraudulent transactions."	The umbrella term for digital currencies, like Bitcoin, that are rooted in the science of cryptography.
Blockchain	"A digital database containing information (such as records of financial transactions) that can be simultaneously used and shared within a large decentralized, publicly accessible network."	An evolution in computer science that allows any type of transaction to be recorded permanently and across a distributed network. It stores, records, and verifies information. Whatever the future of our money looks like, it's likely that blockchain technology will play a part.
Bitcoin	"A digital currency created for use in peer-to-peer online transactions."	Currently, the most prominent digital currency that allows us to make fully digital and secure transactions.

Mine	"To create or obtain more units of (a cryptocurrency) through a cryptographic process."	The process of writing code, across a distributed ledger, to build the blockchain. In other words, the process by which more Bitcoin (and other cryptocurrencies) are released into the digital universe—the blockchain equivalent of printing more money.
Distributed Ledger	"A database that is consensually shared and synchronized across a network spread across multiple sites, institutions or geographies. It allows transactions to have public 'witnesses,' thereby making a cyberattack more difficult."[2]	The database that records all blockchain happenings, ensuring security and accuracy.
Initial Coin Offering (ICO)	"The first sale of a cryptocurrency to the public conducted for the purpose of raising funds (as to support a start-up)."	A novel method for people to raise money for their new project by offering coins or tokens, which fundamentally bypasses a venture or typical angel investing process. It's like the Kickstarter or GoFundMe of the crypto space. ICOs have been significantly overhyped in the news, and we should proceed with caution.
Cryptography	"The computerized encoding and decoding of information."	Highly sophisticated puzzles that protect information.
Ether	"[A cryptocurrency] traded as a digital currency exchange . . . and used inside Ethereum to run applications and even to monetize work."[3]	A cryptocurrency that runs on Ethereum (which is simply a blockchain platform). Ether is second in popularity only to Bitcoin.

THE BYZANTINE GENERALS' PROBLEM

As this new crypto language starts to seep in, let's dig into a blockchain history lesson. As far as stories go, it's a good one—involving a decades-long unsolved riddle, a mysterious inventor whose true identity has never been revealed, and a technological revolution that is changing the world. If it weren't true, you would think I was making it up.

(Note: If the history of blockchain sparks your curiosity, there are some great resources out there that tell a fuller story. Check out Andreessen Horowitz's "Crypto Canon," Nathaniel Popper's *Digital Gold*, Michael J. Casey and Paul Vigna's *Truth Machine: The Blockchain and the Future of Everything*, and the documentary *Banking on Bitcoin* on Netflix.)

Let's start with the unsolved riddle. The "Byzantine Generals' Problem," as it was named in 1982, was a computer science problem that had stumped the software world's smartest minds. Bear with me . . .

Imagine this: A number of Byzantine generals surround a city. They all have to reach a consensus around whether to attack or retreat, but they don't trust each other. If just one general goes his own way, everyone will fail.[4] The solution to this deceptively complex problem was a strategy that is guaranteed to succeed under every possible eventuality.

Fast-forward twenty-six years. The Byzantine Generals' Problem was still considered all but unsolvable. Then, in late 2008, an elusive figure who went by the alias Satoshi Nakamoto published a paper.[5] In it, he described the solution to the puzzle, and it was the logic behind this solution that laid the foundation for blockchain.

As the *MIT Technology Review* explains, "Nakamoto combined established cryptography tools with methods derived from decades of computer science research to enable a public network of participants who don't necessarily trust each other to agree, over and over, that a shared accounting ledger reflects the truth."[6]

In other words, Nakamoto's ingenious breakthrough in cryptography (a subset of computer science) enabled the establishment of a digital database that can facilitate trusted and secure transactions without the oversight of any central authority. To continue the Byzantine Generals' analogy, Nakamoto's solution would allow the generals to reach a consensus while ensuring that there were no traitors and that everyone was planning to act as a unified front. It was dubbed "blockchain," a reference to the growing list of records of transactions, called blocks.

Here's a closer look at how it works:

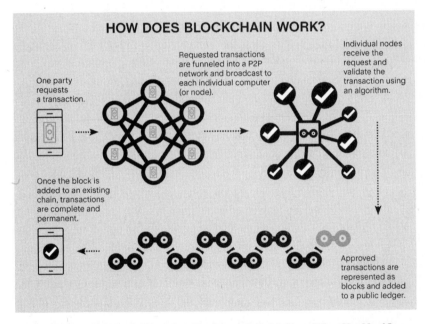

HOW DOES BLOCKCHAIN WORK?

One party requests a transaction.

Requested transactions are funneled into a P2P network and broadcast to each individual computer (or node).

Individual nodes receive the request and validate the transaction using an algorithm.

Once the block is added to an existing chain, transactions are complete and permanent.

Approved transactions are represented as blocks and added to a public ledger.

Source: Stephen Shankland, "Blockchain Explained: It Builds Trust When You Need It Most," *CNET*, February 12, 2018, https://www.cnet.com/news/blockchain-explained-builds-trust-when-you-need-it-most

This blockchain technology became the foundation of the code for Bitcoin, which Nakamoto unveiled shortly thereafter.[7] (If you're wondering where Ethereum fits in, it's just another type of cryptocurrency, akin to Bitcoin, that was released in 2015.) With that code, released on January 3, 2009, he ignited the cryptocurrency revolution that has since taken the world by storm.

So to be clear, blockchain is the underlying technological innovation, and Bitcoin is a cryptocurrency that runs on top of this technology.

To this day, Nakamoto's identity remains under wraps. A number of journalists have zeroed in on possible candidates, from a computer science student from Ireland (Michael Clear) to a trio who filed a patent in 2008 that used similar language to Nakamoto's definitive Bitcoin white paper (Neal King, Vladimir Oksman, and Charles Bry), but all have denied being the inventor or inventors.[8]

WHY DID BITCOIN TAKE OFF?

Mysterious identity aside, Nakamoto's timing was impeccable. The winter of 2009 marked the height of the Great Recession. Lehman Brothers had filed for bankruptcy, the financial system was in turmoil, and trust in the "too big to fail" banks—and the lawmakers who had voted to bail them out—was the lowest it had been in decades. The promise of a completely decentralized currency that operated outside the purview of both Washington and Wall Street was too seductive to resist.

In the early days, Bitcoin was closely associated with the dark corners of the internet. Why? For every new technology, there's the concept of a "killer app," or what *PC Magazine* defines as "a software application that is exceptionally useful or exciting. Killer apps are innovative and often represent the first of a new breed."[9]

You might have heard of Silk Road, the online marketplace that promised anonymity and enabled access to drugs, weapons, and just about anything else that was against the law. (Silk Road was infamously shut down by the FBI in 2013.) To be crystal clear, I'm not condoning Silk Road and the nefarious activities that took place there, but many experts believe that Silk Road was the "killer app" that raised the profile of blockchain and Bitcoin. The fact that Bitcoin was anonymous made it the obvious currency of choice for those transacting in an illegal marketplace. In its heyday, Silk Road took in more than 9.5 million Bitcoins (or $1.3 billion in 2013 value).[10] When a technology scales and is pounded on by tons of users, it either breaks or improves. Silk Road helped blockchain to do the latter; it had to evolve for the better in order to survive.

BITCOIN'S WILD RIDE

Bitcoin has come a long way since its days as anonymous currency used on Silk Road. In just a decade, cryptocurrencies have come out of the shadows of the deep internet and are now entering our mainstream consciousness.

To say that public curiosity in Bitcoin has skyrocketed is an understatement. It went from being an obscure concept known only among small, tech-forward inner circles in 2009, to the number two trending topic on Google in 2017.[11] That year, it was the ninth-most-read article on all of *Wikipedia,* garnering over fifteen million views.[12] And media coverage kept climbing: In June 2017, there were 630 articles published with "Bitcoin" in the title. By November, that number had jumped to 3,788; that's over a 500 percent increase in just five months.[13] Naturally, social media buzz followed, with over six million Bitcoin-related social posts in Q4 of 2017.[14]

Bitcoin headlines made big promises and bold claims: "How Digital Currency Will Change the World,"[15] "Everyone Is Getting Hilariously Rich and You're Not,"[16] "Bitcoin Is a Delusion That Could Conquer the World,"[17] and "Why Bitcoin Is the Investment of the Decade"[18]—to name just a few.

But these buzzy headlines turned out to be more than just empty hype. Alex Rampell, a general partner at the venture capital firm Andreessen Horowitz, claims that Bitcoin now has tens of millions of acolytes worldwide. Among them are Christine Lagarde, managing director of the International Monetary Fund, who said, "It would not be wise to dismiss crypto-assets; we must welcome their potential but also recognize their risks";[19] the investor Tim Draper, who posited, "Cryptocurrencies will eventually replace credit cards and will be something you can access on your phone";[20] the former chairman of Alphabet Inc. (the parent company to Google), Eric Schmidt, who recognized that Bitcoin "is a remarkable cryptographic achievement," adding that "the ability to create something which is not duplicable in the digital world has enormous value."[21] Perhaps Tyler Winklevoss, co-founder of the digital asset platform Gemini, put it best when he eloquently said, "[With Bitcoin] we have elected to put our money and faith in a mathematical framework that is free of politics and human error."[22]

Not everyone is buying it, though. Major names in finance have spoken out against the craze, and many leading economists think Bitcoin is in a major bubble, including Nouriel Roubini, who called Bitcoin "the biggest bubble in human history."[23] Furthermore, Bill Gates said, "I would short it if there was an easy way to do it."[24]

So with all of these conflicting opinions, how should we think about the value of Bitcoin? The numbers surrounding cryptocurrency are quite staggering.

Throughout 2017, the market price of Bitcoin saw an insane upward climb. At the beginning of the year, the price of Bitcoin started around $1,000 and peaked at $19,738.21 on December 17, 2017.[25]

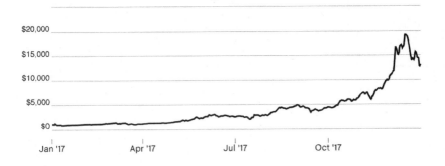

Source: CoinDesk (Price in U.S. dollars from January 1, 2017, to December 31, 2017)

Some crazy stats to consider: In May 2017, one Bitcoin was worth more than *twice* as much as an ounce of gold.[26] By October, Bitcoin reached a market cap of $88.35 billion, which surpassed massive corporations, like Starbucks and American Express.[27] And by December, Bitcoin's total value was $277 billion—almost as large as the economy of Singapore.[28]

Fast-forward to May 2018: Coinbase—a digital currency exchange where people can hold or trade their Bitcoin (and other cryptocurrencies)—opened up its twenty millionth account. For perspective, that far exceeds the number of accounts Charles Schwab has under management and comes close to Fidelity and Vanguard—behemoths in our existing financial system.[29]

Mary Meeker highlighted the growth of Coinbase users in her well-known annual *Internet Trends Report 2018*:

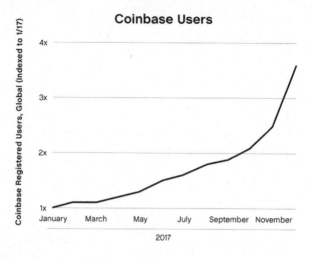

And Coinbase is not the only digital currency exchange out there. Unsurprisingly, many other companies have popped up in the space, including Circle, Blockchain, and Ripple.

Not only has the number of individual investors been on the rise, so has venture capital: from January to May 2018, VCs invested $1.3 billion in blockchain and blockchain-adjacent start-ups, according to an analysis by *TechCrunch*.[30] With so much money flowing in, many think we're past the point of no return when it comes to Bitcoin.

OKAY, BUT WHAT DOES THAT MEAN FOR ME?

To start, please don't immediately run out and buy it. In many ways, the Bitcoin craze is similar to the dot-com boom of 2000, in that there are very real technological advancements happening but also a significant hype machine demanding extreme caution. Buying into the Bitcoin hype—which seemed to peak in 2017—could be dangerous for the everyday investor, particularly one who doesn't fully understand the world of crypto (which is most of us) and who isn't focusing full-time on the changes happening every day in this space.

With so much media buzz surrounding newly minted Bitcoin millionaires, though, it's no surprise that a 2017 survey found that 27 percent of millennials would rather own Bitcoin than stocks.[31] But no asset can continue to rise in value forever, and in 2018, Bitcoin experienced some pretty drastic swings. Remember that December 2017 peak of nearly $20,000? In June 2018, the price of Bitcoin dropped to $5,755,[32] and by November 2018, it fell below $4,000.[33]

That's why I included a warning at the beginning of this chapter. Generally speaking, buying Bitcoin is not a golden ticket. Nor is it a substitute for a financial plan. (As a friendly reminder, for most Americans the most important place to put your extra money is into one of three places—retirement, emergency savings, or paying off credit card debt!) It's simply an early new form of currency—one that could become ubiquitous and used for everyday transactions, or at least one that foreshadows what the digital future of money might look like. While many believe that we might not be too far off from Bitcoin becoming truly mainstream (some estimate this will happen within five years), the tremendous volatility of Bitcoin's value means it's not yet something for consumers to bank on.

That said, Bitcoin is the first cryptocurrency that's truly driving change in how we conceive of the very nature of money. I think there are a number of ways blockchain, which Bitcoin relies on, will impact our future wallets individually—but more on that in the next chapter.

WILL BITCOIN STICK AROUND?

Among the cryptocurrencies that exist thanks to blockchain, there are a few features of Bitcoin that make its longevity seem possible.

Wences Casares, a talented technology entrepreneur who among other roles sits on the board of PayPal, pointed out in an interview that everything in technology runs on "protocols"—just another way of saying standard ways of doing things—and protocols are hard to change. For example, we have only one protocol for email; as he said, it's not particularly great, but it was globally adopted, so we still all use it. Thanks to Bitcoin's first-mover advantage, he believes that Bitcoin will be the most widely adopted crypto protocol.

Another reason it might stick around? Bitcoin was built with limits in place. There can only ever be twenty-one million Bitcoins, but the value of each Bitcoin is what fluctuates. This meets the "scarcity" characteristic of money that we talked about in chapter 1. The U.S. government only prints a certain amount, and that's it. As an interesting side note, the production of those Bitcoins is still in progress! But the algorithm that controls how new Bitcoins are mined is designed to slow down how many are released over time, ensuring that Bitcoin—not unlike gold or diamonds—remains relatively scarce. Taking the future pace of production into account, experts predict that it will take until 2140 to mine the last Bitcoin, which means new Bitcoins will enter circulation for the next century and beyond.[34]

Third, Bitcoin sits on top of the blockchain ecosystem, which has an incentive structure built into it. Remember, blockchain is code that is constantly being written and updated to store more transactions on the distributed ledger. The engineers writing this code are called miners, and anytime a miner records a transaction on the ledger, that miner is compensated in a small amount of Bitcoin for his or her work.

Hopefully, you now have a sense of what's behind the hype, so let's shift gears toward looking ahead at how these foundational technologies could powerfully change the future of money.

CHAPTER 12

THE FUTURE OF THE CRYPTO UNIVERSE

None of us can predict the future. But we can do our best to get smart about what it *may* look like. That's the goal of this chapter.

I've read every crypto-related text I could get my hands on, watched dozens of videos, interviewed countless industry leaders, and talked to the leading entrepreneurs in the space—all with an eye toward taking a balanced, informed approach to the possibilities ahead.

It's easy to exaggerate the potential of blockchain. There is no silver bullet for the future, and I don't believe that one technology can solve all of our problems. I love how simply Wences Casares put it in an interview with me. "I think blockchain will be powerful for the future, and in a few very specific-use cases it will be truly transformative." Ken Lin echoed this sentiment: "I think the tech is fascinating. I don't think it's the panacea that everyone is making it out to be. But there are certain applications of it that I think will be fundamentally transformative."

So the question is, *where* will it be transformative, and what will that look like?

THE SPEED OF CHANGE

As of this writing in late 2018, blockchain is showing early progress toward disrupting the worlds of technology and business. By 2023, Gartner predicts, we'll hit a pivotal moment of transformation. As Gartner explains, "When a disruptive trend is under way, it can proceed at exponential speed once it gains necessary traction."[1]

There's no question that today we are experiencing an astonishingly rapid pace of change. Technology is disrupting industries, and driving major social shifts, at an increasingly accelerated rate.

Think about it this way: When the internet first emerged in the 1990s, no one could have predicted how it would transform the ways in which we work, live, and communicate. We had no way of knowing, for example, that it would someday allow us to chat, in real time, with people located across several oceans, or stream movies from our living room, or order groceries to be delivered to our doorstep. But while it took the Netflixes, Googles, and Amazons of the world over a decade to become household names, new disruptive technologies are going mainstream more quickly than ever. Take, for example, Uber and Airbnb, which grew at a rate of 417 percent and 259 percent, respectively, from 2014 to 2015—just over five years into the founding of each company.

Even at today's accelerated pace, we have to go through key phases in order to reach this pivotal transformation from a niche product to a mass-market one. Gartner has helpfully summarized the potential phases of blockchain disruption on its "DD Scale," which stands for "Digital Disruption."

As Gartner points out, we're currently on the cusp between DD1 and DD2, moving from the stage where we're still enhancing the underlying blockchain technology to one where we're extending its reach.

Today, the blockchain transformation has only just begun. And once it starts to pick up speed, it has the potential to move fast. Because

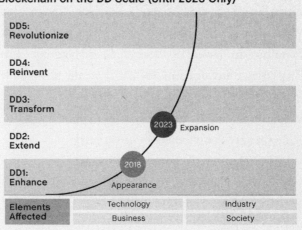

Source: "The Disruptive Potential of Blockchain Technology," Gartner webinar, 2017, https://www.gartner.com/webinar/3805664

here's the thing: blockchain was *designed* to be disruptive. Gartner predicts, "The pattern of disruption will be similar to what occurred with the web, but some expect it to be more pronounced because blockchain, at its core, deals with payment flows and value exchange in a way that the web never did."[2] Gartner predicts that blockchain's business value will reach $176 billion by 2025 and surpass $3 trillion by 2030. It's no longer a question of *if* blockchain will be disruptive, but *when*.

Blythe Masters, CEO of Digital Asset and former JPMorgan Chase executive, believes that "the [blockchain] revolution is in many respects similar to the revolution that was triggered by the invention and popularization of the Internet . . . What we're talking about here is [the possibility of] saving hundreds of billions of dollars of cost and unleashing unprecedented innovation."

Liana Douillet Guzmán, COO of Blockchain, the largest crypto-wallet company, echoes the idea that disruption is coming. "The thing with transformation is that it doesn't happen overnight. It tends to happen little by little and then all at once. We're still in the little-by-little stage and years away from ubiquity, but we are already starting to see the transformational impact this technology will have on individuals and industries across the globe. I believe this technology will completely reengineer the way we transact and exchange value," she predicts, "and has the potential to impact every industry from health care to government, finance to retail, real estate to agriculture, and more."

So let's take a closer look at what changes might be on the horizon, and what this means for each one of our wallets.

FUNDAMENTAL DISRUPTIONS

Even the first set of blockchain-driven disruptions could change how we as individual consumers transact and interact with our money—or as Masters puts it, blockchain could bring "radical improvement in the way value is transferred." Here's what these disruptions look like:

1. NO MORE MIDDLEMEN

Today, when it comes to managing our money (or processing just about any transaction), middlemen abound. There are banks, credit card processors, payment platforms, stock exchanges—the list goes on. Everywhere you look, there are entities standing in between both sides of every transaction we carry out. Oftentimes there are more than just one. And in many cases, one or more of them is taking a cut or charging a fee.

Take a credit card transaction, for example. As a consumer, your money is being handled by both your credit card issuer (for example, Chase) and the payment-processing network (for example, Visa). The store where you make a transaction uses a point-of-sale system (for example, Square) and pays a transaction fee. That's a lot of cooks in the kitchen for one exchange of funds to buy even something as simple as a cup of coffee.

With blockchain, those middlemen could disappear. You'll recall from the last chapter that one of blockchain's main features is that it's decentralized—meaning that you can transact directly with the producer of the item you want to buy, no bank or credit card needed. What that means is that transaction fees on each and every purchase are taken out of the equation. Think about how much money that could put back in your wallet! And more important, think about how much this simplifies the transactions we make—the absence of hidden fees giving us more clarity into where our dollars go.

Marc Andreessen of the venture capital firm Andreessen Horowitz shares a powerful example of what this could mean on a global scale when he describes how people around the world work to send money to family back in their home countries. These workers send $400 billion in total annually, and as he explains, "banks and payment companies extract mind-boggling fees, up to 10 percent and sometimes even higher, to send this money. Switching to Bitcoin, which charges no or very low fees, for these remittance payments will therefore raise the quality of life of migrant workers and their families significantly. In fact, it is hard to think of any one thing that would have a faster and more positive effect on so many people in the world's poorest countries."[3]

2. SMART CONTRACTS

Today, executing a contract is a rigorous process that involves lawyers and headaches. Think about buying a house. You have brokers, real estate lawyers, lawyers from the bank, the deed company; the closing process involves a ton of people and literally mountains of paperwork (and of course, legal fees).

But blockchain can eliminate just about all of it. You don't need all of those records and documents; all the information is stored within the blockchain itself. Buying something like a deed becomes seamless. Contracts can be automated and direct. With the time it takes to buy and sell reduced, property can suddenly become a more liquid and accessible asset for consumers, pushing transaction costs down and allowing consumers to more easily tap into their home equity.

Blockchain, in other words, takes power out of the hands of institutions and puts it into the hands of the consumer. As the multi-time tech entrepreneur and early stage venture investor David Pakman puts it, "Have you ever bought or sold a house and found you had to pay extra for a 'title search'? Why is it so hard to locate the title of a property that clearly indicates who owns it? And have you also had to pay for 'title insurance,' to ensure that the owner actually owned the property they sold you? Both of these 'taxes' on real estate exist because public data has no immutable, trustable, independent place to live. Blockchain offers us a potential solution to tracking ownership of property in a way that removes these inefficiencies and taxes."

3. A MORE SECURE, MORE STREAMLINED WALLET

Let's face it, it's no surprise that so many people fall victim to credit card fraud in today's world. We all know that if someone walks into a store and tries to buy something with your credit card, the cashier is barely even going to glance at the name on the card, let alone the signature, and certainly won't ask for ID in the absence of a signature. The transaction is then sent to your credit card company, where it takes a day or two to fully process. If it was a bigger-than-normal purchase, or perhaps occurred five states away from the one in which you live, the credit card company might assume something is fishy and send you a fraud alert, or perhaps you check your statement a week later and notice that something is wrong. All told, it takes days for a transaction to be tracked and verified as fraudulent, another day or two for your new card (to replace the one you had to cancel) to arrive, and so on.

But all of that could be streamlined with blockchain. Because transaction records are permanent and immutable, there isn't a question about who is involved in a transaction. As Ken Seiff, founder of Blockchange Ventures, explains, our information "will be encrypted in our wallets and backed up in small pieces on thousands of random computers," making fraud virtually impossible. We already know that our phones will soon become our wallets, because they can be protected on so many levels, from fingerprints to facial-recognition software. With blockchain our phones could store not just our credit cards and passwords but our medical records and prescriptions, and even the "keys" to our car and home. Your identity will be fundamentally managed in one spot.

Ryan Alfred, founder of the financial company BrightScope (acquired in 2016) and now the Bitcoin-industry company Framework, agrees that in the future "all of your assets will be held in a single wallet and will be represented by digital tokens that can be transformed into any other asset 24/7/365. Applying for loans, paying bills, investing, will all occur via digital assets stored on global decentralized networks."

With all this information stored in one central database, Seiff, among others, predicts that "we will be rewarded for thousands of small transactions annually. Walk into a store and get paid automatically. Get the same coffee five days in a row and get paid. Rent a car three times and get paid. Like social media has unlocked a new marketing channel over the past decade, the blockchain wallet will unlock a new form of marketing: direct marketing that instantly pays you for actions you take."

Similarly, Marla Blow, founder and CEO of FS Card, adds that our digital wallets will be "so information rich that they will open many, many doors to other opportunities." In other words, rather than a generic 20 percent off Labor Day sale, our favorite companies will be able to incentivize us in ways that really matter to us, putting more money back into our wallets. Sounds like progress to me!

BROADER NEXT-LEVEL DISRUPTIONS

Once these disruptions start to change the way we as individuals interact with money, the next phase will be disruption across industries and society. Here's a taste of what that could look like:

4. MORE CONSUMER-FRIENDLY BUSINESS MODELS ACROSS INDUSTRIES

Right now, we have a sense of the many, many different types of businesses that survive and thrive on the internet. There are too many to name, including subscription services, like Amazon Prime; SaaS (software as a service) companies, like Salesforce; online marketplaces, like Etsy; e-commerce companies, like Wayfair.

But we can't even begin to imagine what business models could emerge out of blockchain. In 2014, Marc Andreessen wrote a seminal article on Bitcoin called "Why Bitcoin Matters." In it, he talks about the possibilities for new businesses and fundamentally new business models that could come out of Bitcoin.

We currently can't fathom a world where consumers pay less than a penny for anything. But Bitcoin currently goes down to eight decimal places, which mean we can divide it into tiny fractions of pennies. Think about what that might mean for how we pay for something like a subscription to *The New York Times,* in which Andreessen's article appears. He explains, "All of a sudden, with Bitcoin, there is an economically viable way to charge arbitrarily small amounts of money per article, or per section, or per hour, or per video play, or per archive access, or per news alert." That potential is transformative for media companies *and* fairer for consumers who pay only for the content they consume. And this is just one small example of how business models may evolve in radical ways that can benefit all of us.

5. A FLATTER AND MORE EQUITABLE GLOBAL ECONOMY

While "globalization" has been a buzzword for decades now, huge economic disparities between countries still exist. Blockchain could play a central role in making a global economy more equitable and more powerful. There are *two billion* people worldwide who are without a single account at any financial institution or bank.[4] That means that this staggering number of people do not currently have safe ways to transfer, save, or efficiently grow their money. For me, it is heartbreaking to think that so many people around the world cannot easily create financial stability for their family.

Michael Carvin, CEO of SmartAsset, believes that the digitization of our wallets "will significantly expand financial options for the un- or under-banked, creating more egalitarian access to the financial system." Furthermore, Casares explains, "Right now, we have a global, nonpolitical standard of weight, length, and temperature, but we do not have one of value. If we had a global, nonpolitical standard, this could be truly revolutionary in how we think about money flowing powerfully across the planet."

Blockchain has the potential to flatten the playing field, ending the advantages that one currency might have over another. Or, as explained by Ryan Alfred, "Everyone, everywhere who has a cell phone and access to the internet will have access to the entire financial system—not just banking and borrowing, but also investing in any asset around the world in any increment with minimal fees." Imagine the benefits of this for billions of people.

Another interesting prediction is the potential to use blockchain to introduce a universal basic income. Currently, cost and complexity are two of the main obstacles to providing every human on the planet with some minimum level of resources to fund their well-being. But what if we could directly transfer funds to someone in need without any sort of infrastructure obstructing the process?

In a recent *Fast Company* article, Harriet von Froreich, who leads communication at the blockchain company Circle, explains, "Money is not a god or a force of nature; it's a tool, a societal agreement. Instead of a top-down distribution, it could be created at the hands of people directly—for example, through code. So why not create and distribute money fairly by giving the same amount to every account in a system?"[5]

Such a proposal is relevant not only on the global scale but also right at home—in our own local communities. In this new world, you could support any political or social cause, anywhere, almost instantly. That means everything from helping starving children or refugees in danger around the world, to contributing to local hurricane relief or supporting a neighbor whose home burned in a fire. Your money could go straight to people in acute crisis, near or far, with frictionless ease.

Imagine the poverty we could end, the suffering we could prevent, and the stability we could create?

But while blockchain holds the potential to put more and more power into the hands of individuals, that doesn't mean it's going to be easy.

"The future of crypto must be simplicity," explained Spencer Lazar, a partner at General Catalyst. "The technology has so many incredible benefits to corporations, consumers, and governments. But it is still too complicated for most people to grasp and integrate into their daily lives. Because of the profundity of what's possible with it, we need it to succeed. But to do so, it will need to be simple."

These new technologies are endlessly complex, but the possibility for innovation is endless, too.

When I think about the shape our future will take, I love to imagine what's possible.

As someone who cares deeply about helping everyone in America and across the globe live better and more financially secure lives, I could not be more excited to see how the next decade unfolds. And while I don't claim to be able to see into the future, I think it's safe to assume that over this next decade, a few big things will happen:

▷ The major trends transforming our wallets will continue to touch all of our lives. We will start to take more advantage of these new modes of living, working, earning, and spending that are now available to us.

▷ As our working years extend beyond the traditional retirement age (and full "retirement" becomes more rare), the gig economy will become a critical tool in supplementing our income and increasing our earning potential.

▷ Ownership will continue to decrease as the ultimate financial priority. By embracing the sharing economy, we'll hold on to more money and shift how we save and invest toward other goals.

▷ Everyday tools are popping up to help us get better clarity in our wallets and control over our money (see page 184 for the best current apps to download). As consumers, we will continue to have more choice than ever to use technology to effect positive change.

▷ Going cashless—and even cardless—will become less of a preference and more of the norm as our smartphones become our wallets.

▷ Because money is just a tool to reach our goals, our ability to put our finances on autopilot—and still stick to a smart financial plan—will improve. Just as generations used to stash money under their mattresses, we'll take advantage of the myriad places to "stash" our money online and keep it working for us.

▷ Best practices for keeping our money secure will evolve, and we must evolve with them.

▷ Our children, as digital natives, will live in a very different world when it comes to money. The more prepared we are for the changes ahead, the more we can prepare them to thrive.

▷ Our foundational advancements in technology, namely blockchain, will be transformative across industries and produce new innovations that will positively impact how society functions.

Financial planning is all about looking ahead. It's thinking about what you want your future to look like and making sure that your money will get you there. Yes, change can be intimidating. When it comes to money—just like with anything else—we have to keep learning, keep feeling hopeful, and stay positive about the future to ensure that we're leveraging the best of what's available to us and living our own richest lives.

My hope is that you've learned a new trick (or five) to organize and optimize your money, that you feel confident in embracing the tools technology has to offer, and most important that you, too, are excited by the many ways in which we're evolving as a society.

At my core, I am an optimist. I believe that if we look to the future with a positive mind-set—and a major dose of practicality and planning—these technologies can create a better world for us all. I recognize that all innovation, while bringing tremendous advancements, can also bring unforeseen challenges, setbacks, and hiccups. And I believe that technology can also help us overcome them. As a mom with little kids, I am hopeful about all that these advancements could do for future generations—while moving our world financially forward, together.

GLOSSARY OF APPS

Note: The following represent some of the top apps in their category as of the writing of this book. I've selected these based on a variety of factors, from their ease of use to their market dominance. As a FinTech investor, I do invest in a number of apps I love, and I've marked all of my investments with an asterisk for full disclosure!

GIG ECONOMY AND ON-DEMAND

I've grouped these because they represent platforms that you can both use as a consumer and leverage as a gig worker.

ALFRED—modern butler service that handles everything from dry cleaning to grocery shopping

BLUE APRON—ingredient-and-recipe meal kit service that delivers pre-portioned meals to you

CARE.COM—platform to find care professionals, specializing in child care and senior care

DOORDASH—restaurant food delivery, on demand

FIVERR—freelance marketplace, with an emphasis on design, digital marketing, and video

GLAMSQUAD—on-demand, in-home beauty services

GRUBHUB—like DoorDash, restaurant food delivery, on demand

HANDY—housecleaning and handyman services

INSTACART—local on-demand grocery delivery

JETBLACK—personal shopping via text message

LYFT—on-demand transportation company, where rides are just a tap away

PLATED—ingredient-and-recipe meal kit service, now owned by Albertsons

POSTMATES—deliveries from local restaurants and stores

ROVER—pet care marketplace, from pet sitting to dog walking

TASKRABBIT—book or offer handyman or home services, like furniture assembly

*UBER—like Lyft, on-demand transportation company, where rides are just a tap away

*UMBRELLA—membership service that provides help around the house for those over sixty-five years old

UPWORK—network of freelancers, enables people to find, hire, work, and pay on one platform

URBANSITTER—platform to find babysitters and nannies

ZEEL—on-demand, in-home massages

SHARING ECONOMY

Platforms that help you borrow or get more value out of the things you already own.

AIRBNB—book and list vacation properties and experiences

APTDECO—buy and sell secondhand furniture

GETAROUND—peer-to-peer car-sharing company

HOMEAWAY—like Airbnb, book and list vacation properties

POSHMARK—digital marketplace to buy and sell clothing

RENT THE RUNWAY UNLIMITED—a subscription to designer fashion

SPOTHERO—find or rent a parking space

THE REALREAL—online luxury consignment sales

TRADESY—like Poshmark, digital marketplace to buy and sell clothing

TURO—like Getaround, a peer-to-peer car-sharing company

VRBO (VACATION RENTALS BY OWNER)—like Airbnb, book and list vacation
  properties

ZIPCAR—car-sharing platform

MONEY MANAGEMENT

Tools to help you organize, check in, and save.

ALBERT—puts your budget and financial plan on autopilot

CLARITY MONEY—budgeting tracker that also helps manage subscriptions

CREDIT KARMA—check your credit score, credit reports, and monitoring

CREDIT SESAME—like Credit Karma, check your credit score, credit reports,
  and monitoring

DIGIT—analyzes your spending to help you automatically save

EMPOWER—financial assistant app

LEVEL—budgeting app that tells you how much you can afford to spend daily

MINT—all-in-one budgeting app, with built-in credit score checks

NERDWALLET—track spending and check your credit score

PERSONAL CAPITAL—see all of your accounts in one spot

PRISM—track bills and pay them seamlessly

QAPITAL—a bank account designed to help you save for goals

TRUEBILL—manage subscriptions and lower your bills

WALLY—daily expense tracking

YOU NEED A BUDGET (YNAB)—budgeting program based on the envelope
  method, where spending is divided into categories

DEBT MANAGEMENT

Platforms that help with everything from credit cards to student loans.

COMMONBOND—refinance student loans

EARNEST—like CommonBond, refinance student loans

SOFI—refinance student loans, mortgages, and more

*TALLY—pay down credit card debt faster

INVESTING

Tools to help your money grow.

ACORNS—automatically invests your spare change

BETTERMENT—financial adviser that helps you invest

ELLEVEST—goal-based investing designed for women

MOTIF—select investments based on your values

ROBINHOOD—no-fee stock trading

STASH—learn how to invest and do it easily

WISEBANYAN—builds and manages your investment plan

INSURANCE

InsureTech companies working to make insurance coverage an easier process.

CLOVER—health insurance offering, particularly focused on elderly and
low-income patients

COVER—helps you find and manage renter's, home, and car insurance

ETHOS—offers term life insurance policies

FABRIC—like Ethos, offers term life insurance policies

*LADDER—like Ethos, offers term life insurance policies

*LEMONADE—renter's and home insurance, selected via chatbot

OSCAR—direct-to-consumer health insurance company

POLICYGENIUS—marketplace to compare and buy life insurance

PEER-TO-PEER

How to transact and manage money with others.

CASH—easily transfer money between phones

PAYPAL—receive and send money to PayPal users

SPLITWISE—easily split expenses with friends

VENMO—make and share payments with friends

ZELLE—directly send and receive money

SECURITY

Protect your financial information and your family.

DASHLANE—password management app

FAMILYTIME—manage parental controls and screen time

KEEPER—like Dashlane, password management app

LASTPASS—like Dashlane, password management app

NET NANNY—set restrictions and parental controls

ACKNOWLEDGMENTS

My life has changed and grown immeasurably since the publication of *Financially Fearless* in 2013. In the past few years, Northwestern Mutual purchased LearnVest; I took on the role of Chief Innovation Officer for the company, and, most significantly, I became a mom to beautiful children, which truly grounds you in the most unimaginable and humbling of ways.

I now know the importance of "It takes a village," and the value of having a whip-smart executive assistant in Ashley Greenberg, who helps keep me on track. I am incredibly grateful to the many people in my life who support, challenge, and inspire me every day.

To the Penguin Random House team—I owe a debt of gratitude to Talia Krohn for pushing my ideas forward, editing with clarity, and bringing joy to the book process.

Tina Constable, Campbell Wharton, Ayelet Gruenspecht, and Megan Perritt, thank you for believing in me and being such a pleasure to work with on *Financially Fearless* and now *Financially Forward*.

To my team at William Morris Endeavor—Andy McNicol, Suzanne Lyon, Bethany Dick, Julie Leventhal, Strand Conover, Jason Hodes, and Marissa Hurwitz—thank you for believing in me over the years and helping me share this mission of financial literacy and empowerment with the world.

To Annie Shapiro—you are a joy! Meeting you nine years ago as the first LearnVest intern and working so closely together has been one of the most fulfilling parts of my career. I relish our partnership and look forward to a lifetime of many more exciting projects. Thank you for always diving into work with positivity and your brilliant mind!

To Sunshine Sachs—Dani Dalesandro, you're phenomenal to work with and an even better friend. I am so lucky for our decade of friendship. Shawn Sachs, you are a remarkable strategist and sounding board. Thank you both for being such a special part of my journey.

To the Northwestern Mutual family—thank you for the incredible partnership, not only for our marriage to LearnVest but also for sharing the sincere belief in empowering Americans to take control of their wallets. In particular, John Schlifske, you are a visionary, unyielding in your commitment to reimagining a client's financial life but also in your unwavering effort to accomplish the best for your policyholders. A special thanks to Christian Mitchell, who has been a best friend and the rock behind the LearnVest acquisition; to Ron Joelson and Sheldon Cuffie for letting me tap their brains; and to the entire Northwestern Mutual senior leadership team: Mike Carter, Jo Eisenhart, Tim Gerend, Aditi Gokhale, John Grogan, Ron Joelson, Ray Manista, Christian Mitchell, Beth Rodenhuis, Tim Schaefer, and Emilia Sherifova.

To Ann Kaplan, Theresia Gouw, John and Maria Chrin, and Lee Barba—my passion for financial literacy has deep roots, and you have been tremendous cheerleaders and mentors from the beginning. You've shared such wisdom with me, not only about running a business but also about living a rich and fulfilling life. Thank you!

To all of the experts who so generously gave their time and wisdom on where the future of money might take us—I value our relationships and am so grateful you've shared your perspectives. Thanks to, in alphabetical order, Ryan Alfred, Jake Anderson-Bialis, Marla Blow, Jason Brown, Stacy Brown-Philpot, Michael Carvin, Wences Casares, Liana Douillet Guzmán, Jennifer Hyman, Kim Kingsley, Spencer Lazar, Sam Lessin, Ken Lin, Blythe Masters, Rebecca Minkoff, Max Motschwiller, Michael Norton, Daphne Oz, David Pakman, Matt Salzberg, Daniel Schreiber, Ken Seiff, Jon Stein, Danielle Weisberg, Melanie Whelan, Tyler Winklevoss, Carly Zakin, and Randi Zuckerberg.

To Mark Batsiyan, Dan Wagner, and Natasha Duré for your incredibly thoughtful and diligent feedback on my many drafts of this book. I value each of you so much.

And last but most certainly not least, to my best friends (you know who you are!!!) and family for driving me forward in every inch of my life. To my mom, stepdad, and brothers, Travis and Brandon, for believing in me and continuing our family legacy of service to others. To Mike, Patricia, Bonnie, and James for being wonderful in-laws and grandparents. To Cliff, thank you for your continual and tireless encouragement as a partner, husband, and now father to our beautiful children, Toby and Cashel.

NOTES

INTRODUCTION

1. PWC, *Redrawing the Lines: FinTech's Growing Influence on Financial Services,* Global FinTech Report 2017, www.pwc.com.

2. Deloitte, *Fintech by the Numbers: Incumbents, Startups, Investors Adapt to Maturing Ecosystem,* Deloitte Center for Financial Services, 2017, www2 .deloitte.com.

CHAPTER 1: BUT FIRST, WHAT IS MONEY?

1. "The Properties of Money," Money Project, money.visualcapitalist.com; "Functions of Money," *The Economic Lowdown* (podcast), episode 9, Federal Reserve Bank of St. Louis, www.stlouisfed.org.

2. "Functions and Characteristics of Money: A Lesson to Accompany *The Federal Reserve and You,*" Federal Reserve Bank of Philadelphia, 2013, www .philadelphiafed.org.

3. "Barter System History: The Past and Present," *Mint,* www.mint.com.

4. Chapurukha Kusimba, "Making Cents of Currency's Ancient Rise," *Smithsonian,* June 20, 2017, www.smithsonianmag.com.

5. "What Is Money?," *Investopedia,* May 31, 2018, www.investopedia.com.

6. Sharon Ann Murphy, "Early American Colonists Had a Cash Problem. Here's How They Solved It," *Time,* Feb. 27, 2017, time.com.

7. Neale Godfrey, "A Few Words About Bitcoin . . . Because Fiat Is Not Just a Car," *Forbes,* May 8, 2015, www.forbes.com.

8. "What Is Money?," *Investopedia.*

9. Ibid.; "From the Colonies to the Twenty-First Century: The History of American Currency," U.S. Currency Education Program, www.uscurrency .gov; "The Diners Club Legacy," Diners Club International, www.diners club.com; Claire Tsosie, "What the First Credit Cards Were Like," *Nerd-Wallet,* Aug. 31, 2016, www.nerdwallet.com; Suzanne McGee and Heidi Moore, "Women's Rights and Their Money," *Guardian,* Aug. 11, 2014, www .theguardian.com; "About Venmo," Venmo, venmo.com; "What We Do," World Bank, www.worldbank.org; PYMNTS, "Throwback Thursday: Pay-Pal's Biggest Days in History," PYMNTS.com, July 2, 2015, www.pymnts .com; "Apple Pay Set to Transform Mobile Payments Starting October 20," Apple, press release, Oct. 14, 2014, www.apple.com; "Creating the Consumer Bureau," Consumer Financial Protection Bureau, www.consumer finance.gov.

CHAPTER 2: SIX TRENDS CHANGING OUR WALLETS

1. For Alexa, see the Capital One website: www.capitalone.com.

2. "Longevity and Retirement," *Fidelity Viewpoints,* March 16, 2018, www .fidelity.com. Emphasis added.

3. National Center of Health Statistics, "Longevity in the United States, 2016," NCHS Data Brief, no. 293 (Dec. 2017), www.cdc.gov.

4. "Americans Are Living Longer," USC Leonard David School of Gerontol-ogy, gerontology.usc.edu.

5. "Underestimating Years in Retirement," Stanford Center on Longevity, longevity.stanford.edu.

6. "Retirement & Survivors Benefits: Life Expectancy Calculator," Social Se-curity Administration, www.ssa.gov.

7. "Age 65 Retirement," Frequently Asked Questions, Social Security Admin-istration, www.ssa.gov.

8. "Benefits Planner: Retirement," Social Security Administration, www.ssa.gov.

9. *Planning & Progress Study 2018,* Northwestern Mutual, news.northwestern mutual.com.

10. Ben Steverman, "Working Past 70: Americans Can't Seem to Retire," *Bloomberg,* July 10, 2017, www.bloomberg.com.

11. "2017 Retirement Confidence Survey—2017 Results," Employee Benefit Research Institute, www.ebri.org.

12. "Longevity and Retirement."

13. Mitra Toossi and Elka Torpey, "Older Workers: Labor Force Trends and Career Options," Bureau of Labor Statistics, *Career Outlook,* May 2017, www.bls.gov; Roger St. Pierre, "How Older Entrepreneurs Can Turn Age to Their Advantage," *Entrepreneur,* May 26, 2017, www.entrepreneur.com.

14. Jason Zweig, "Meet 'Future You.' Like What You See?," *Wall Street Journal,* March 26, 2011, www.wsj.com.

15. "Historical Marital Status Tables," U.S. Census Bureau, Nov. 2017, www.census.gov.

16. Macaela MacKenzie, "This Is the Average Age of Marriage Right Now," *Women's Health,* March 26, 2018, www.womenshealthmag.com.

17. "Table 1600. Number of Earners in Consumer Unit: Annual Expenditure Means, Shares, Standard Errors, and Coefficients of Variation," Consumer Expenditure Survey, 2016, Bureau of Labor Statistics, Aug. 2017, www.bls.gov.

18. Assumes annual contributions of $6,954 and 5 percent interest. Compound Interest Calculator, Moneychimp, www.moneychimp.com.

19. "Infertility," Centers for Disease Control/National Center for Health Statistics, July 15, 2016, www.cdc.gov; Laura Lyons Cole, "A Single Round of Fertility Treatments Can Cost over $20,000—a Couple Who Did It Breaks Down Where the Money Went," *Business Insider,* June 25, 2017, www.businessinsider.com.

20. "Families Projected to Spend an Average of $233,610 Raising a Child Born in 2015," U.S. Department of Agriculture, press release no. 0004.17, Jan. 9, 2017, www.usda.gov.

21. Kellie Bancalari, "Private College Tuition Is Rising Faster Than Inflation . . . Again," *USA Today,* June 9, 2017, www.usatoday.com.

22. Genworth, "Compare Long Term Care Costs Across the United States," Genworth 2017 Cost of Care Survey, www.genworth.com.

23. *Guide to Long-Term Care Insurance,* America's Health Insurance Plans, 2013, www.ahip.org.

24. Freelancers Union, *Freelancing in America: A National Survey of the New Workforce,* Freelancers Union & Elance-oDesk, fu-web-storage-prod.s3.amazonaws.com.

25. Betterment, *Betterment's 2018 Report: Gig Economy and the Future of Retirement,* www.betterment.com.

26. Elizabeth O'Brien, "Retirees Are Making Friends—and Money—with This New Handyman Service Created by Millennials," *Money,* Aug. 20, 2018, time.com.

27. Guy Berger, "Will This Year's College Grads Job-Hop More Than Previous Grads?," *Linkedin Official Blog,* April 12, 2016, blog.linkedin.com.

28. "Does Job Hopping Help or Hurt Your Career?," Robert Half, April 5, 2018, rh-us.mediaroom.com.

29. "Poll Finds 80 Percent of Workers in Their 20s Want to Change Careers," Reuters, July 1, 2013, www.huffingtonpost.com.

30. Lesley Vox, "Debunking 5 Myths About Changing Careers in Your 50s," *Forbes,* June 21, 2017, www.forbes.com.

31. Stefan Sagmeister, "The Power of Time Off," TED Global 2009, July 2009, www.ted.com.

32. Shawn Achor and Michelle Gielan, "The Data-Driven Case for Vacation," *Harvard Business Review,* July 13, 2016, hbr.org.

33. "2017 Employee Benefits: Remaining Competitive in a Challenging Talent Marketplace," Society for Human Resource Management, June 2017, www.shrm.org.

34. Kathryn Vasel, "This Company Just Started Offering 6-Week Sabbaticals," *CNN Money,* Jan. 27, 2017, money.cnn.com; Schwab 2016 Employee Guide, Charles Schwab, 2016, www.aboutschwab.com.

35. "100 Best Companies to Work For," *Fortune,* 2018, fortune.com.

36. Dina Gerdeman, "Want to Be Happier? Spend Some Money on Avoiding Household Chores," *Harvard Business School Working Knowledge,* Nov. 13, 2017, hbswk.hbs.edu.

37. Aaron Smith and Monica Anderson, "Online Shopping and E-commerce," Pew Research Center, Dec. 19, 2016, www.pewinternet.org.

38. Aaron Smith, "Other Shared and On-Demand Services," Pew Research Center, May 19, 2016, www.pewinternet.org.

39. Charles Colby and Kelly Bell, "The On-Demand Economy Is Growing, and Not Just for the Young and Wealthy," *Harvard Business Review,* April 14, 2016, hbr.org.

40. Lisa Gevelber, "Micro-moments Now: Why Expectations for 'Right Now' Are on the Rise," *Think with Google,* Aug. 2017, www.thinkwithgoogle.com.

41. Colby and Bell, "On-Demand Economy Is Growing."

42. Bryan Walsh, "Today's Smart Choice: Don't Own. Share," *Time,* March 17, 2011, content.time.com.

43. Maya Kosoff, "Why Airbnb Is Now Almost Twice as Valuable as Hilton," *Hive,* March 10, 2017, www.vanityfair.com.

44. Shira Springer, "Why Is It So Hard to Stop Buying More Stuff?," *Boston Globe Magazine,* May 18, 2017, www.bostonglobe.com.

45. Fleura Bardhi and Giana M. Eckhardt, "Access-Based Consumption: The Case of Car Sharing," *Journal of Consumer Research* 39, no. 4 (Dec. 2012): 881–98.

46. "Millennials: Fueling the Experience Economy," Eventbrite, eventbrite-s3 .s3.amazonaws.com.

47. Judith Wallenstein and Urvesh Shelat, "Hopping Aboard the Sharing Economy," BCG Henderson Institute, Aug. 22, 2017, www.bcg.com.

CHAPTER 3: THE FINANCIAL FOUNDATION EVERYONE NEEDS

1. Monique Morrissey, *The State of American Retirement: How 401(k)s Have Failed Most Americans,* Economic Policy Institute, March 3, 2016, www.epi.org; Lee Barney, "Americans on Track to Replace 64% of Income in Retirement," *PLANADVISER,* April 26, 2018, www.planadviser.com.

2. "Missing Out: Are You Saving Enough to Receive Your Employer's 401(k) Savings Match?," Financial Engines, financialengines.com.

3. Heather Gillers, Anne Tergesen, and Leslie Scism, "A Generation of Americans Is Entering Old Age the Least Prepared in Decades," *Wall Street Journal,* June 22, 2018, www.wsj.com.

4. Gabrielle Olya, "Here's How the Average Savings Account Interest Rate Compares to Yours," GOBankingRates, Aug. 20, 2018, www.gobanking rates.com; Kelly Dilworth, "Rate Survey: Average Card APR Remains at Record High of 16.32 Percent," CreditCards.com, Jan. 10, 2018, www.credit cards.com.

5. Consumer Financial Protection Bureau, *Consumer Experiences with Debt Collection: Findings from the CFPB's Survey of Consumer Views on Debt,* Jan. 2017, s3.amazonaws.com.

6. "How Much Is Renters Insurance?," PolicyGenius, www.policygenius.com.

7. Ellen Stark, "5 Things You Should Know About Long-Term Care Insurance," *AARP Bulletin,* March 2018, www.aarp.org.

8. James Royal, "What Is the Average Stock Market Return?," *NerdWallet,*
    Feb. 28, 2018, www.nerdwallet.com.

CHAPTER 4: MAINTAIN GOOD MONEY HABITS

1. Charles Duhigg, "How to Create a Habit," charlesduhigg.com.

CHAPTER 5: HACK 1—ONLY HAVE THE ACCOUNTS YOU NEED

1. Cameron Huddleston, "50% of Americans Are Cheating—on Their Bank,"
    GOBankingRates, www.gobankingrates.com.
2. Olya, "Here's How the Average Savings Account Interest Rate Compares to
    Yours."
3. Dayana Yochim, "Best Online Brokers for Stock Trading 2018," *NerdWallet,*
    Jan. 9, 2018, www.nerdwallet.com.
4. "U.S. Employers Enhancing Defined Contribution Retirement Plans to
    Help Improve Workers' Financial Security," Willis Towers Watson, press
    release, Feb. 26, 2018, www.willistowerswatson.com.

CHAPTER 7: HACK 3—YOUR DAILY WALLET

1. Kevin Purdy, "Baby Photos Might Get Your Lost Wallet Returned," *Life-
    hacker,* July 13, 2009, lifehacker.com.
2. Art Swift and Steve Ander, "Americans Using Cash Less Compared with
    Five Years Ago," Gallup, July 12, 2016, news.gallup.com.
3. "Digital Payment Platforms Primed to Topple Cash," U.S. Bank, news re-
    lease, Aug. 16, 2017, www.usbank.com.
4. Claire Tsosie, "The History of the Credit Card," *NerdWallet,* Feb. 9, 2017,
    www.nerdwallet.com.
5. "Digital Payment Platforms Primed to Topple Cash."
6. Ellen A. Merry, "Mobile Banking: A Closer Look at Survey Measures,"
    Federal Reserve, March 27, 2018, www.federalreserve.gov.
7. *Consumers and Mobile Financial Services 2016,* Federal Reserve, March 2016,
    www.federalreserve.gov.
8. Dan O'Shea, "Study: Consumer Adoption of Major Mobile Payment Apps
    Stalls," *Retail Dive,* March 19, 2017, www.retaildive.com.

9. "Cashless Made Effortless," Apple, www.apple.com.

10. David Phelan, "How to Use Apple Pay on iPhone: The Complete Guide for Reluctant Users," *Forbes*, June 19, 2018, www.forbes.com.

11. Alex Morrell, "You No Longer Need a Card to Get Cash from Nearly Every Chase ATM," *Business Insider*, Aug. 4, 2018, www.businessinsider.com.

12. Mobile Fact Sheet, Pew Research Center, Feb. 5, 2018, www.pewinternet .org.

13. Alex Samuely, "Mobile Boarding Passes to Number 1.5 Billion by 2019: Report," *Retail Dive*, www.retaildive.com.

14. *Credit Card Processing Fees and Rates Explained*, Square, squareup.com.

15. Matthew Cochrane, "Why Venmo Is So Popular with Millennials," *Motley Fool*, March 22, 2017, www.fool.com.

16. Sarah Perez, "U.S. Banks' Venmo Alternative, Zelle, Moved $75B Last Year, Says 100,000 People Enroll Today," *TechCrunch*, Jan. 29, 2018, tech crunch.com.

17. Aaron Pressman, "Venmo Battles Bank Copycats by Adding a Much-Desired New Feature," *Fortune*, June 25, 2018, fortune.com.

18. Kam Leung Yeung, "Exploring the Origin of Pain of Payment in Cash and Its Relevance to Computer Payment Interface" (PhD diss., Iowa State University, 2014), lib.dr.iastate.edu.

19. Austin Carr, "How Square Register's UI Guilts You into Leaving Tips," *Fast Company*, Dec. 12, 2013, www.fastcompany.com.

20. Dan Ariely, "The Pain of Paying: The Psychology of Money," Fuqua Faculty Conversations, Jan. 14, 2013, events.fuqua.duke.edu.

CHAPTER 8: HACK 4—SMART SHOPPING

1. "New Research Shows 60% of U.S. Adults Made Amazon Purchase in Past Three Months," *Convenience Store News*, Sept. 18, 2017, csnews.com.

CHAPTER 9: HACK 5—PROTECTING YOUR HARD-EARNED CASH

1. Aaron Smith, "Americans and Cybersecurity," Pew Research Center, Jan. 26, 2017, www.pewinternet.org.

2. David Gewirtz, "The Best Password Managers for 2018," *CNET*, Feb. 16, 2018, www.cnet.com.

3. Julie Bawden Davis, "Password Security: 9 Tips for Safeguarding Your Company's Sensitive Data," American Express OPEN Forum, July 14, 2017, www.americanexpress.com.

4. Nate Lord, "101 Data Protection Tips: How to Keep Your Passwords, Financial & Personal Information Safe," Digital Guardian, Sept. 19, 2018, digitalguardian.com.

5. "Wireless Connections and Bluetooth Security Tips," Federal Communications Commission, Oct. 20, 2017, www.fcc.gov.

6. Elizabeth Weise, "Equifax Breach: Is It the Biggest Data Breach?," *USA Today*, Sept. 7, 2017, www.usatoday.com.

7. Seena Gressin, "The Equifax Data Breach: What to Do," Federal Trade Commission, Sept. 8, 2017, www.consumer.ftc.gov.

8. Associated Press, "Equifax Finds Its Big Data Breach Hit an Additional 2.4 Million People," *Los Angeles Times,* March 1, 2018, www.latimes.com.

9. Paul Roberts, "Equifax Hacked via Six Month Old Struts Vulnerability," Digital Guardian, Sept. 14, 2017, digitalguardian.com.

10. John Patrick Pullen, "What You Should Do This Weekend to Protect Your Credit from the Equifax Data Breach," *Fortune,* Sept. 15, 2017, fortune.com.

11. Lisa Weintraub Schifferle, "Equifax Isn't Calling," Federal Trade Commission, Sept. 14, 2017, www.consumer.ftc.gov.

12. "Place a Fraud Alert," Federal Trade Commission, Sept. 2018, www.consumer.ftc.gov.

CHAPTER 10: HACK 6 — RAISING DIGITAL WALLET NATIVES

1. "New Research Shows Children Form Attitudes About Money at Young Age," Michigan Ross, Jan. 10, 2018, michiganross.umich.edu.

CHAPTER 11: DECODING BLOCKCHAIN

1. "The Dictionary Just Got a Whole Lot Bigger," *Merriam-Webster,* March 2018, www.merriam-webster.com.

2. "Distributed Ledgers," *Investopedia,* www.investopedia.com.

3. "Ethereum," *Investopedia,* www.investopedia.com.

4. Georgios Konstantopoulos, "Understanding Blockchain Fundamentals, Part 1: Byzantine Fault Tolerance," *Medium,* Nov. 30, 2017, medium.com.

5. Satoshi Nakamoto, "Re: Bitcoin P2P E-cash Paper," Nov. 13, 2008, www
    .mail-archive.com.

6. "Explainer: What Is a Blockchain?," *MIT Technology Review*, April 23,
    2018, www.technologyreview.com.

7. Joshua Davis, "The Crypto-currency," *New Yorker*, Oct. 10, 2011, www
    .newyorker.com.

8. Adam L. Penenberg, "The Bitcoin Crypto-currency Mystery Reopened,"
    Fast Company, Oct. 11, 2011, www.fastcompany.com.

9. *PC Mag* Encyclopedia, s.v. "killer app," www.pcmag.com.

10. "Are You Ready for Blockchain?," Thomson Reuters, www.thomsonreuters
    .com.

11. Year in Search 2017, Google Trends, trends.google.com.

12. "The Top 50 Report—2017," *Wikipedia*, en.wikipedia.org.

13. Will Gannon, "Analyzing the Media Coverage of Bitcoin—November
    Monthly Media Review with the AYLIEN News API," *AYLIEN*, Dec. 7,
    2017, blog.aylien.com.

14. "Bitcoin Social Conversation Is Mirroring Its Close Price," *Crimson Post*,
    Dec. 21, 2017, www.crimsonhexagon.com.

15. Brian Armstrong, "How Digital Currency Will Change the World," *The
    Coinbase Blog*, Aug. 31, 2016, blog.coinbase.com.

16. Nellie Bowles, "Everyone Is Getting Hilariously Rich and You're Not," *New
    York Times*, Jan. 13, 2018, www.nytimes.com.

17. Derek Thompson, "Bitcoin Is a Delusion That Could Conquer the World,"
    Atlantic, Nov. 30, 2017, www.theatlantic.com.

18. "Why Bitcoin Is the Investment of the Decade," *Seeking Alpha*, Sept. 5, 2017,
    seekingalpha.com.

19. Richard Partington, "'Fight Fire with Fire': IMF's Lagarde Calls for Bitcoin
    Crackdown," *Guardian*, March 13, 2018, www.theguardian.com.

20. Rachel Wolfson, "Tim Draper on the Future of Cryptocurrency, His New
    Book, and Why Bitcoin Will Hit $250,000 by 2022," *Forbes*, May 2, 2018,
    www.forbes.com.

21. "Bitcoin Bulls and Bears: Who's Hot, Who's Not on Crypto," *Bloomberg*,
    Oct. 2, 2018, www.bloomberg.com.

22. Nathaniel Popper and Peter Lattman, "Never Mind Facebook; Winklevoss
    Twins Rule in Digital Money," *DealBook* (blog), *New York Times*, April 11,
    2013, dealbook.nytimes.com.

23. Joanna Ossinger, "Roubini Says Bitcoin Is the 'Biggest Bubble in Human
    History,'" *Bloomberg*, Feb. 2, 2018, www.bloomberg.com.

24. Kate Rooney, "Bitcoin Almost Broke Through the $10,000 Mark—Then Warren Buffett and Bill Gates Came Along," *CNBC*, May 7, 2018, www.cnbc.com.

25. Kieran Corcoran, "Bitcoin Is Climbing on the Last Day of 2017," *Business Insider*, Dec. 31, 2017, www.businessinsider.com.

26. "One Bitcoin Is Worth Twice as Much as an Ounce of Gold," *Economist*, May 25, 2017, www.economist.com.

27. Jessica Marmor Shaw and Ryan Vlastelica, "Literally Just One Massive Chart That Says Everything About Bitcoin in 2017," *MarketWatch*, Oct. 12, 2017, www.marketwatch.com.

28. "Are You Ready for Blockchain?," Thomson Reuters, www.thomsonreuters.com.

29. Brian Fung, "Move Deliberately, Fix Things: How Coinbase Is Building a Cryptocurrency Empire," *Washington Post*, May 17, 2018, www.washingtonpost.com.

30. Jason Rowley, "With at Least $1.3 Billion Invested Globally in 2018, VC Funding for Blockchain Blows Past 2017 Totals," *TechCrunch*, May 20, 2018, techcrunch.com.

31. Spencer Bogart, "7 Stats That Highlight a Millennial Propensity for Bitcoin," *Forbes*, Nov. 8, 2017, www.forbes.com.

32. Brad Tuttle, "Bitcoin Just Hit a New Low for 2018. Here's How Much You Would Have Lost If You Bought at the Peak," *Money*, June 25, 2018, time.com.

33. "Bitcoin Falls Further Below $4,000," *Fortune*, Nov. 25, 2018, fortune.com.

34. Matthew Frankel, "6 Jaw-Dropping Stats About Bitcoin," *The Motley Fool*, Dec. 10, 2017, www.fool.com.

CHAPTER 12: THE FUTURE OF THE CRYPTO UNIVERSE

1. Ray Valdes, "The Disruptive Potential of Blockchain Technology," Gartner Webinar, 2017.

2. Ibid.

3. Marc Andreessen, "Why Bitcoin Matters," *DealBook* (blog), *New York Times*, Jan. 21, 2014, dealbook.nytimes.com.

4. Irina Asktrakhan, "2 Billion People Worldwide Are Unbanked—Here's How to Change This," World Economic Forum, May 17, 2016, www.weforum.org.

5. DJ Pangburn, "With This Cryptocurrency, Everyone Gets Paid," *Fast Company*, April 18, 2018, www.fastcompany.com.

INDEX

ABOUT THE AUTHOR

Alexa von Tobel, CFP®, is founder and managing partner of Inspired Capital and the *New York Times*–bestselling author of *Financially Fearless*.

Prior to Inspired Capital, Alexa founded LearnVest in 2008 with the goal of helping people make progress on their money.

After raising nearly $75 million in venture capital, LearnVest was acquired by Northwestern Mutual in May 2015 in one of the biggest FinTech acquisitions of the decade. Following the acquisition, Alexa joined the management team of Northwestern Mutual as the company's first-ever chief digital officer, overseeing digital strategy. She later assumed the role of chief innovation officer, through which she oversaw Northwestern Mutual's venture arm.

Alexa has appeared on the cover of *Forbes*, been interviewed on NPR's *How I Built This*, and been featured in a wide variety of publications, ranging from the *New York Times* to *Vogue*. She is a member of the 2016 Class of Henry Crown Fellows and an inaugural member of President Barack Obama's Ambassadors for Global Entrepreneurship. Alexa has been honored with numerous recognitions, including *Fortune*'s 40 Under 40, *Fortune*'s Most Powerful Women, *Forbes*'s 30 Under 30, *Inc.*'s 30 Under 30, and the World Economic Forum's Young Global Leader.

Originally from Florida, Alexa attended Harvard College and Harvard Business School before settling in New York City, where she currently resides with her husband, Cliff Ryan, and their soon-to-be three children.

MASTER THE **FINANCIAL PLAN** THAT LETS YOU BE YOU, **ONLY RICHER.**

"Financial planning just got more accessible."

—*Wall Street Journal*

"Geared to help the financially complacent and those who need a push to face their finances . . . [*Financially Fearless*] delivers sound suggestions in an easy-to-digest package."

—*Success*